Living in Style

Architecture + Interiors

Chris van Uffelen

Living in Style

Architecture + Interiors

BRAUN

CONTENTS

PREFACE

Living in Style – everybody wants to live in Style. The number of magazines that focus on this topic is never-ending, not to mention blogs, webpages, catalogues in furniture stores, advertisements and Hollywood films; and now there is also this book. You might ask what the point of such a publication is, when there is already so much material about this topic. Well, a book doesn't just present six examples like a magazine might, and can't be altered and changed at will like a website. It is also more objective than a manufacturer's catalogue and doesn't just form the background for something else like a Hollywood film.

A book takes a much more in-depth look at a subject and although it makes a selection, the selection is much more varied and still relevant years later. Despite this, such a book cannot reasonably be called timeless: This book presents projects from the last five years; current projects that are not just relevant at the moment, but also for a lon-

ger period of time – these are not projects that have been quickly decorated and will be redecorated in a couple of years, but are rather spaces where the residents want to make a financial investment in the decoration that should last and one day might even be considered design classics.

This compilation demonstrates current style. For example, a lot of the projects are predominantly white and bright and have three chairs in the kitchen. Despite this, the book still offers a varied representation of projects that go against white, minimalist design in a way that only a book can. Projects characterized by warm, dark tones also have their place in this volume: For example, warm colors juxtaposed with large glazed openings or encased in a protective wooden envelope. Libraries show the client's thirst for knowledge, while fitness rooms hint at a love of movement. Dining halls speak of a desire to entertain and cozy dining/kitchen areas suggest a longing for

comfy social gatherings. The designs cover everything from single-story apartments and bungalows, to houses and villas of all sizes. Some are concentrated over just 50 square meters, while others are spread out over an area ten times the size. They tell stories of single or family life, all over the world, from northern regions to the tropics.

This publication is a compendium of private and semi-private projects, built in the second decade of the 21st century, and thus a spatial representation of modern cul-

ture. Most of the rooms are empty of people, but it doesn't require much imagination to be able to picture them, because there are so many traces of them in the images; whether a scattering of toys left lying around, the selection of books in the library or on a bookshelf, or the owners own personal art or photography collection.

Professional architects and interior designers have carried out the designs in this volume. Over 100 examples clearly demonstrate the interplay between spatial boundaries and furnishings and the important roles that both play in the development of space. This book focuses neither on pure interior design nor architecture, but rather on how these two entities fuse together to form a coherent whole, supporting not just everyday life but also special days and events.

The texts introduce the readers to the ideas behind the designs. They describe the clients' specific demands or problematic questions that arose during the project development; although some of the spotlight texts also focus on one specific design aspect. The texts and clearly presented facts help to explain the individual concept ideas behind the designs. The rooms tucked between the pages of this book are unique and often feature customized and tailor-made solutions; although that doesn't mean that many of them can't be used as inspiration for a new or different design.

The division of the rooms is often imaginative. For example, a living room separated from the dining area with an eccentric shelf, or contrasting materials can be used to define different zones. Transitions from one room to the next can be unified by connecting surfaces, or similar colors – proving that anyone can live in style.

23.2 HOUSE

Untamed forest meets the hand of man. 100-year-old Douglas fir beams form the heart of this house.

Architect | Omer Arbel Office (OAO)
Gross floor area | 326 m²
Address | 936-184th street Surrey, Vancouver V3S 9R9, Canada
Completion | 2010
Number of residents | 2 adults, 3 children

23.2 is a house built on a rural site, situated between masses of old growth forest. The design forms two distinct outdoor spaces, each with a distinct ecology and lighting conditions. The starting point for the design was a depository of 100-year-old reclaimed Douglas fir beams which were treated as sacred artifacts, remaining uncut and unfinished. Due to variations in size and length, a triangular geometry was used to accommodate the dimensional difference of the beams. By pulling the structure away from the corners and using a folding door system, the entire façade on both sides disappears in order to blur the boundary between interior and exterior space.

93 m² living
15 m² sleeping
23 m² kitchen
22 m² mudroom
30 m² playroom
17 m² entrance area

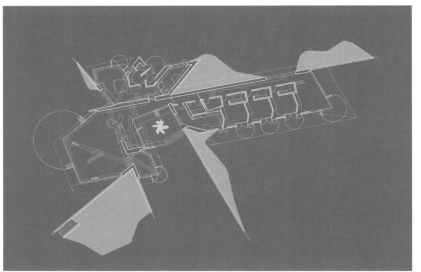

100-year-old reclaimed Douglas fir beams in varying shapes and sizes form the centerpiece of this house. They have retained their original rough appearance and the design works around them, retaining their unique character.

LOFT ESN

An Alice in Wonderland living landscape of floating lighting elements, kitchen units stacked like building blocks, fluffy carpets and mirrored walls.

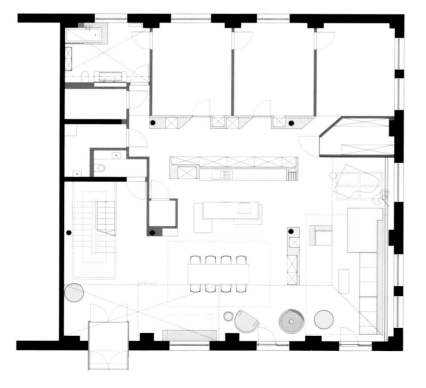

80.5 m² living
82 m² sleeping
17.75 m² kitchen
45.5 m² bathrooms
25 m² entrance area

Interior design | Ippolito Fleitz Group – Identity Architects
Gross floor area | 347.5 m²
Address | Esslingen, Germany
Completion | 2012
Number of residents | 2 adults, 2 children

As one enters this loft, the room opens out not only horizontally but also vertically. The living and entrance areas are separated by just an L-shaped curtain partition. The dining area is the central focus of the design. The open kitchen is characterized by the arrangement of stacked cubes and rectangles. A sliding partition separates the living and dining areas. The upper floor is reserved for the parents. A house-in-a-house concept houses the bedroom because the client desired a completely dark space. The floating light drops in the bedroom illuminate the space and connect the collage-like objects and rooms to form a poetic landscape.

Warm natural materials and colors, including dark parquet flooring, the earthy tones of the walls and curtains, as well as gold surfaces are carefully complimented with pink sections, cubes of mineral materials or glazed surfaces.

TRAVELER'S TALE

Ernest Hemingway pointed out that it is not the getting somewhere that matters in the end, but the journey. Turns out he was right.

Done

MONSTER

NAOKI URASAWA Volume 1

Architect | goodnova godiniaux
Interior design | goodnova godiniaux
Co-architect | Julia Orlova
Gross floor area | 145 m²
Address | Moscow, Russia
Completion | 2013
Number of residents | 2 adults

This project is a traveler's tale about a globetrotter who decided to put down his suitcases in Moscow. Right from the outset, the architectural desire to accentuate the light washing through was a key idea and beyond this, the idea of travel acted as an inspiration. A module was born, in the middle of a rectangle that concentrates all the functions, separates the rooms one from another and allows the design to break free of corridors and reduce the amount of furniture. Clad in a single material, it provides continuity and consistency while the rooms that gravitate around it have their own decoration. Like a giant trunk left lying there, it's different faces open on to the entrance hall, and on to the kitchen and living room. In the bedroom, a mirror is incorporated that faces the open dressing room.

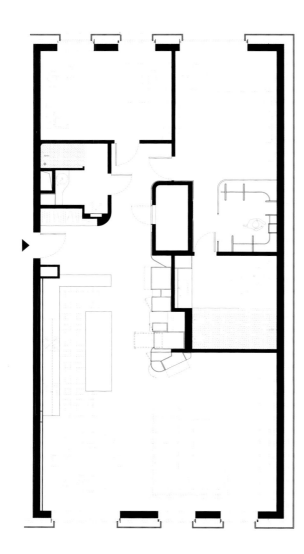

55 m² living
25 m² sleeping
13 m² kitchen
18 m² bathrooms
7 m² corridors
16 m² office

Nine suitcases welcome the visitor right from the entrance. Designed in Paris by the architects and built by some Portuguese craftsmen from a little town near Porto they are made with mutene timber, covered with different kinds of leather and are an obvious reference to the client's nomadic way of life. They already travelled half of the world and nothing is preventing the client from taking them off again.

JOINT-FAMILY PENTHOUSE

Colors aren't just colors, they show attitude –
something this house has in masses.

The clients of this penthouse are a family of two brothers, their respective wives and children, and their parents. The intent of the design was to break this typological context into a more personal and customized one. All the walls were broken and repositioned. Cutouts were made to join the floors and develop changes in the basic volume. The staircase is fashioned in such a way that it becomes a space for gathering and discussion. Two incisions are made to connect the upstairs and the downstairs areas, from where the brothers can overlook and engage into the dialogue of the house. The yellow wall, the wood and the clearly defined upstairs are each derived from the plural nature of the family members and coexist just like a family.

Architect | Gaurav Roy Choudhury
Gross floor area | 297 m²
Address | Malleswaram, Bangalore, India
Completion | 2013
Number of residents | 6 adults, 3 children

The colors were chosen to complement the moods of the different areas. The yellow reflects the warmth and the playfulness of the activities in the lower spaces. The blue was chosen to create a contrast to the yellow near the children's play area. The wood and soft tones used upstairs emphasize the use of this area as a private space in which one can relax.

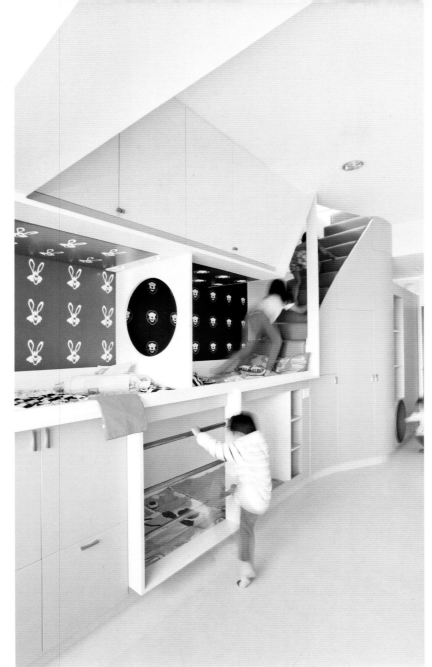

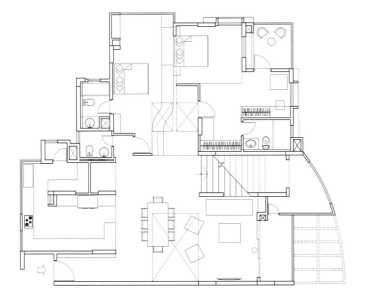

13.5 m² living
29 m² dining
71 m² sleeping
14.5 m² kitchen

25

GS HOUSE

Brazilian colonialism meets modern magnificence.

Architect | Jacobsen Arquitetura
Interior design | Jacobsen Arquitetura
Gross floor area | 1,190 m²
Address | Itu, São Paulo, Brazil
Completion | 2013
Number of residents | 2 adults, 2 children

A striking feature of this house is the garden at its center. This appears as part of the house design, rather than as a separate entity, added as an afterthought. The arrangement draws light deep into the house, casting a soft glow over the stylish furnishings. The house is a modern country home, but with a Brazilian essence. The wooden furnishings inside complement the materials used for the exterior. The warm colors and soft lighting give the house a friendly and welcoming appearance. Large windows and sliding doors aid orientation and allow uninterrupted views throughout the space.

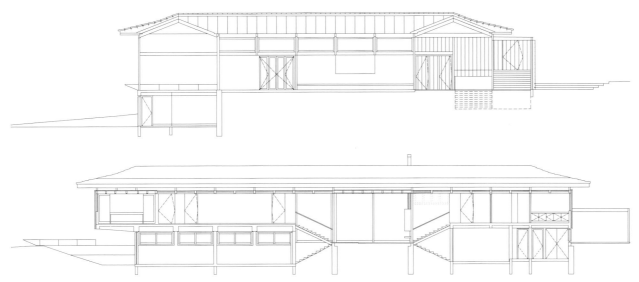

149 m² living
172.65 m² sleeping
33.5 m² kitchen
3.5 m² bathrooms
25 m² office

The contradiction of colonial Brazilian vocabulary with the contemporary concepts of architecture creates a striking and welcoming home with a modern accent. Tiles, stonewalls, wooden structures, shutters, rough granite floors and floorboards coexist with double-height ceilings, large glass doors, and suspended floors that are independent of the slender structure.

COUNTRY HOME IN DORES DO INDAIÁ

Living in the lap of luxury: what more do you need?

Architect | Gislene Lopes Arquitetura e Design de Interiores
Interior design | Gislene Lopes Arquitetura e Design de Interiores
Landscape architect | Junia Lobo
Gross floor area | 1,322.5 m²
Address | Minas Gerais, Brazil
Completion | 2012
Number of residents | 6 adults, 2 children

This country house in Dores do Indaiá is a family home and the clients demanded a design that would tell the story of the location and yet still be contemporary and elegant. The large overhanging roof and the choice of materials share a dialogue with traditional Brazilian architecture. The lower floor is divided into a service area, dining room, porches and living area, connected to the outdoor area and pool via a covered walkway. Upstairs the bedrooms are connected to the outside balconies, taking full advantage of the stunning views.

This house also includes a small brick chapel. Incisions on either sides of the entrance form a cross shape, where the light streams out in the evening.

133.6 m² living
142.7 m² sleeping
144,1 m² kitchen
52.3 m² bathrooms
190.6 m² porch
53.8 m² home cinema

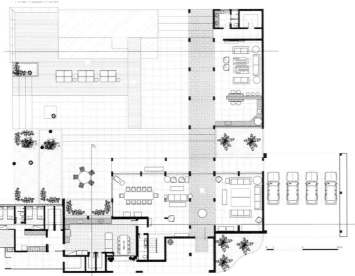

N.B.K. RESIDENCE

Living on the edge. This project pushes the boundaries between present und future, real and unreal, dark and light.

Architect | Bernard Khoury / DW5
Gross floor area | 600 m²
Address | 9th Floor, 10, Habib Pasha Al Saad Street, Beirut, Lebanon
Completion | 2013
Number of residents | 2 adults, 2 children

This three-story apartment is articulated through an independent structure capping the building. Structurally, the apartment only shares the building's vertical circulation core, as well as the perimeter along which the two peripheral walls lie. The apartment comprises three levels. The mezzanine level accommodates two additional bedrooms, as well as the continuation of the floor-to-ceiling library accessible at this level by a steel bridge crossing the entire frame of the reception. Two antennae containing light fixtures crown the outdoor pool terrace on the roof. Oriented towards the south, these projections exceed the height average of the adjacent buildings, making them visible from the surrounding neighborhoods.

80 m² living
130 m² sleeping
17 m² kitchen
8 m² bathrooms
50 m² library
60 m² guest room

An extremely dense hood-like structure, designed in coordination with a mechanical engineer, dominates the ceiling in the main room. This is clad with black plaster, a traditional material typically associated with ornamental cornices and moldings. However, in this case the plaster is painted black rather than white and portrays a much more contemporary and machinist expression. The result is an alien-like object that seems to hover above the space.

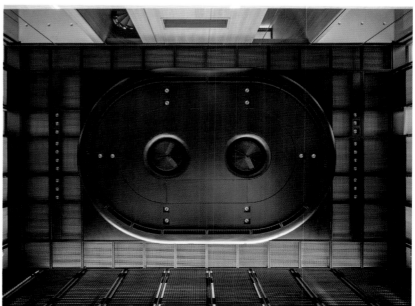

CHALET BRIGELS

A new and modern Alpine lifestyle flourishes in the heart of the Swiss mountains.

Interior design | Go Interiors
Gross floor area | 291.5 m²
Address | Brigels, Switzerland
Completion | 2013
Number of residents | 2 adults

This project involved transforming two apartments located above each other, into one single Alpine living experience for a married couple and their two dogs. The entire design was based on the idea of modern chalet style with a tendency towards eclecticism. The traditional architectural style of the Tarcisi Maissen's company was combined with modern elements to create the perfect living environment. Traditional 'Alpine' materials were used but were newly interpreted to emphasize the modernity of the design. A high level of detail and high-quality materials characterize the house. The design concept, lighting design, materials and colors, decorative elements and textiles were chosen to suit the specific requirements of the space.

The extensive use of timber design elements reflects the Alpine surroundings.

51.3 m² living
54.2 m² sleeping
11.4 m² kitchen
32.9 m² bathrooms
21 m² fitness

The primary organizational element of the interior is the kitchen. Embedded within the simple post and beam structure, the kitchen was conceived as a programmatic block that the architects 'carved out' in order to contribute to both a sense of function and organization. In conjunction to the porous programmatic kitchen block as a connective element, the walls along the main corridor add to the sense of bringing the outside inside. The living, kitchen and dining areas are all connected by a walnut veneer feature wall running the length of the house. This wall echoes the lush surroundings of Lucas valley as well as the original mahogany plywood panels used.

24.03 m² living
35.75 m² sleeping
16.42 m² kitchen
17.7 m² bathrooms

APPLEBERRY DRIVE RESIDENCE

New life has been breathed into this jewel of modernism.

Architect | building Lab
Gross floor area | 146 m²
Address | Appleberry Drive, San Rafael, CA, USA
Completion | 2014
Number of residents | 2 adults, 1 child

THE BARNACLE

A bit like camping, but much, much better.

Architect | Built-Environment Practice
Gross floor area | 35 m²
Address | Broken Head Road, 2481 Byron Bay, Australia
Completion | 2011
Number of residents | 2 adults

The Barnacle is a compact extension to an existing residence, programmed to provide space for sleeping, bathing, writing, and sitting in the winter sun. The project is designed to deliver a maximum of experience within limiting constraints. Evoking the sensation of camping, or berthing in the belly of a yacht, the project requires active participation by the occupant to open, close, and adjust built-in elements to control light, privacy, storage, and ventilation. A built-in bed with concealed lighting hovers in the center of the space, around which a hoop-pine wrapper of storage, desk space, and framed views are orchestrated. The palette of materials includes copper cladding, glass, hoop pine plywood, and Australian cypress. The result is a small extension to an existing holiday house that creates an additional private sleeping and living space for guests.

Built-in furniture around the bed creates storage space and immediately offers a maximum of comfort.

9 m² deck area
25 m² sleeping
4 m² bathrooms

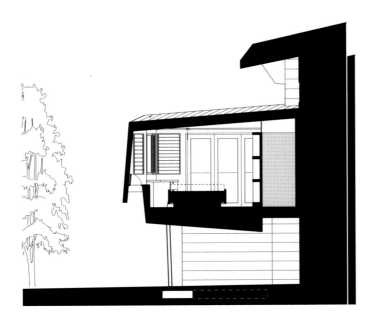

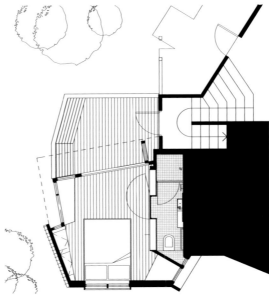

KITCHEN BUNGALOW

A reinterpretation of living in the woods. Here,
a tree shoots up through the middle of the kitchen.

Architect | Ghezzi Novak
Interior design | Ghezzi Novak
Gross floor area | 35 m²
Address | Prolongación Arenales 820, Miraflores, Peru
Completion | 2013
Number of residents | 2 adults

The client required a kitchen and a street access to make his recently subdivided lot habitable once again. The kitchen was placed where an old open-roofed storage room used to be; the existing walls and the tree inside worked as basic, pivotal elements guiding the proposal. Ghezzi Novak decided to create a space where the difference between inside and outside was very clear. This separation of atmospheres reinforces the experience of the interior space, and thus supplies another form of indoor and outdoor relationship to the site. The project served as an exploration of processing natural light and the use of materials in their most essential and primary state.

50

The relation between the interior and the exterior is mainly provided by two openings in the existing walls: one for the kitchen area and another for the dining area. These openings were designed as two pieces of furniture that also serve as windows, whose depth was to be used as shelves or storage spaces. These 'furniture-windows' work as systems that help to control light, ventilation and the outside view, changing the space to the convenience of the people using it.

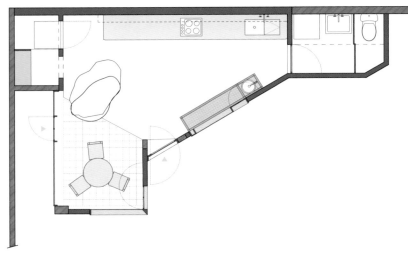

LIENZO DE BARRO

So natural it almost looks like it grew out of the ground, this house is a true eco architecture gem.

Architect | Chaquiñan Taller de Arquitectura
Gross floor area | 219 m²
Address | Tumbaco, Ecuador
Completion | 2013
Number of residents | 2 adults

This project began when a married couple decided to settle in the countryside, in a little house of bamboo and brick. The lack of space meant that a new extension was soon required. The new building was designed to coexist in harmony with the existing house. The volume is oriented towards the sunrise and views are directed over the surrounding countryside. The existing volume houses the private areas, such as the bedrooms, while the new building offers space for cooking, dining and relaxing. The front wall is glazed, which not only helps to illuminate the interior with natural light, but also allows easier temperature regulation.

The most unusual feature of this house is the materials used. Clay bricks and wood give the home a rustic and natural appearance, allowing it to work with, rather than against, the natural environment.

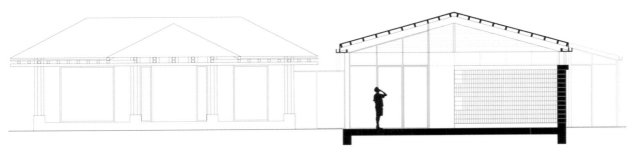

62 m² living
12 m² sleeping
18 m² kitchen
9 m² bathrooms
18 m² hallway

This holiday home is located in the Hallingdal valley. The design was developed for a family of four who required a straightforward program for their mountain lodge: four bedrooms, separate living and dining areas, a lounge, and a mezzanine for the younger children. In addition, a small annex has been created to accommodate guests and visiting grandparents. The architects' response was a cabin of clear and clean-cut expression with a continuous skin of timber cladding on the exterior walls and roof, which will acquire a grey patina with time. The main volume houses mostly bedrooms and follows the natural contours of the landscape, splitting into two living zones. This shift in program and use of multiple levels allow the building to adapt to the slope of the site.

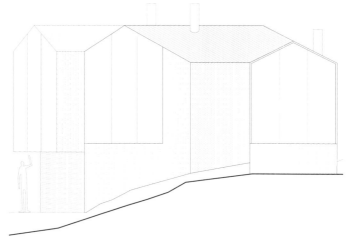

29.9 m² living
20.6 m² sleeping
18.6 m² kitchen
8.8 m² bathrooms
11.3 m² entrance

SPLIT VIEW MOUNTAIN LODGE

Where skiing meets style to form a sophisticated shelter that offers protection from the long and cold Norwegian winter.

Architect | Reiulf Ramstad Arkitekter
Gross floor area | 136.4 m²
Address | Havsdalen, Buskerud, Norway
Completion | 2013
Number of residents | 2 adults, 2 children

Homogenous timber wood cladding was used on the walls, ceilings and floors to create a warm and welcoming atmosphere throughout the house.

LANDHAUS WAGNER

Mister Wagner is watching you.
Pixel art in perfection.

Architect | Architektur am Wasserschlösschen Christa Kelbing
Interior design | Architektur am Wasserschlösschen Christa Kelbing, formade materials
Gross floor area | 904 m²
Address | Klufterner Straße 85, 88048 Friedrichshafen-Spaltenstein, Germany
Completion | 2009
Number of residents | 6 adults, 2 children

According to inventor Joseph Wagner, his portrait in the entrance area was designed as an engineered surface. His image is translated into metal 'pixels', that are individually angled to reflect the light and to cast shadows. The visible portrait is simply built up from that interplay of light and shadow across the surface. The wall was designed in a way that the image can be clearly perceived when entering the house. Upon moving closer the surface turns back into an abstract pattern.

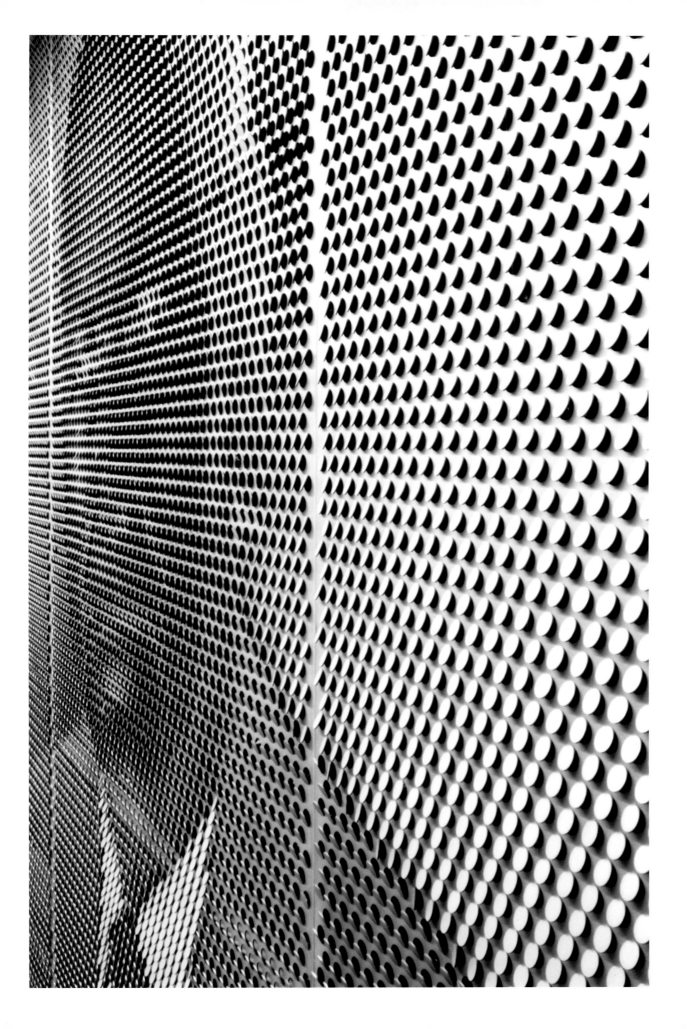

63

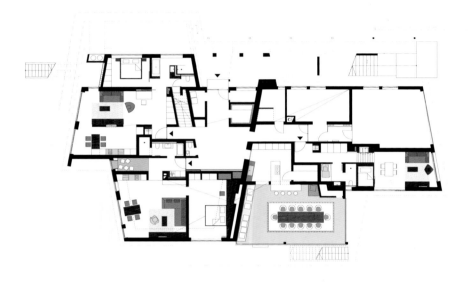

220 m² living
29 m² sleeping
50 m² kitchen
44 m² bathrooms
86 m² office

This country house was built for factory owner Josef Wagner in 1965 according to plans by the architects Schließmann und Sihler. Located near the Lake of Constance, the building is considered an exemplary 1960s architectural monument. As soon as one enters the over 100-square-meter 'salon' it is like being transported back in time to the era of the first James Bond film. The surfaces have been finished with customized materials such as ceramic wall tiles or aluminum relief patterns. The technology used is very unusual for the era in which it was built. Highlights include electrically operated terrace windows and modern home automation systems. Within the framework of the renovation in 2009, the Josef Wagner foundation moved to the upper floor and the former utility rooms at garden level have been transformed into employee apartments. The former swimming pool has been converted into a common dining and meeting room.

This house was designed for a family of four to enhance shared experiences between its members. By opening up visual lines of its interiors the house celebrates social gathering areas and merges with nature. The design is inspired by the idea of a tree house, blurring the lines between interior and exterior yet keeping it safe and protected. The open spaces tie the house together allowing each private room to have its own personality and inviting natural light into the very core of the home.

39 m² living
79 m² sleeping ensuite
36 m² kitchen
30 m² corridors
28 m² entrance area

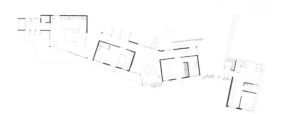

CASA TUSCANIA

High-up, hidden and green – you don't need
a tree house to experience tropical life amongst
the treetops.

Architect | Cincopatasalgato
Gross floor area | 260 m²
Address | San Salvador, El Salvador
Completion | 2007
Number of residents | 2 adults, 2 children

The use of neutral tones and simple furnishings help to emphasize the interaction of architecture and nature. The materials also have a rather 'rough' appearance, which shows their original and unadulterated quality.

This house is located in Del Valle, one of the most traditional neighborhoods in Mexico City. The area enjoys a central location and wide tree-lined streets serving both vehicular and pedestrian access. The design was developed for a young couple and comprises a main level where the social areas are located, with a pleasant living room with a chimney, dining room, bar, wine cellar, kitchen and family room. The bedrooms and a studio are located on the first floor, while the second floor houses the service areas. Part of the house has been extended to the rear, which helps to achieve a better orientation of all the spaces within a highly organized grid.

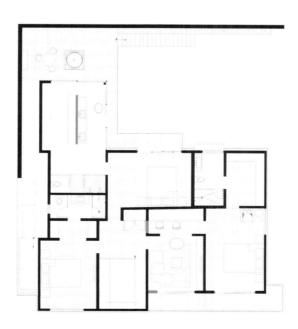

110 m² living
85 m² sleeping
50 m² kitchen
56 m² bathrooms

FATIMA HOUSE

Meditatively modern. Relax in a world where
state-of-the-art and tradition collide.

Architect | Jorge Hernandez de la Garza
Interior design | Abraham Ornelas, Javier Pichardo, Caria Celis
Gross floor area | 650 m²
Address | Del Valle, Mexico City, Mexico
Completion | 2014
Number of residents | 4 adults

The ventilated façade was covered by a NBK ceramic cover, a natural material that gives the house a warm appearance. This house is the first single-family housing project in Mexico covered with this material.

This five-bedroom penthouse house was designed for a married couple and their two teenage daughters. The spatial arrangement was optimized in order to better meet the residents' needs: a modern and timeless appearance that is nevertheless purist in character. Four bathrooms, an open-plan living room with kitchen and a spa area on the lower floor. An intermediate level was added to serve as an office and library. Materials typical of the Alps region were integrated and reinterpreted. The selected materials, the play of light and shadow, as well as the furnishings and colors have all been precisely matched, thus giving the house a sense of harmony and unity.

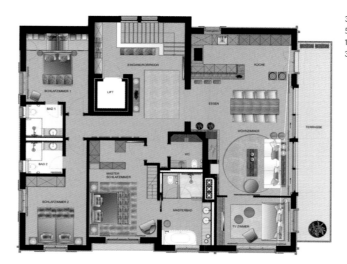

33.3 m² living
57.6 m² sleeping
19.5 m² kitchen
35.6 m² bathrooms

74

KLOSTERS PENTHOUSE

Interior design | Go Interiors
Gross floor area | 270.1 m²
Address | Klosters, Switzerland
Completion | 2013
Number of residents | 2 adults, 2 children

The use of timber beams and complimentary wooden furnishings is what really sets this house apart. The timber roof beams, wooden panels on the walls, and solid wooden furniture successfully create an elegant yet natural space that combines timeless design ideas with modern elements.

THE SIX

Can't decide between the desert and the sea?
Here you'll find both.

Architect | fikrr architects
Co-architect | Fahad Alhumaidi
Gross floor area | 700 m² (2 buildings)
Address | Bnaider, Kuwait
Completion | 2010
Number of residents | 8 adults, 4 children

This home is located in the prestigious Bnaider area in Kuwait. The project involved the construction of six houses and was designed to be completed in three phases. The first phase was successfully completed in 2010 and consists of two houses, located on a 700-square-meter site. Inside, the corridors have hardwood floors, high ceilings and white walls. The interior design is contemporary, and elegant. The arrangement makes the most of the view, with windows to the east and west framing glimpses of the desert and sea. The open-plan ground floor accommodates the living room, dining room, kitchen, utility room and bathroom, while two bedrooms and two bathrooms can be found on the first floor. The interior furnishings are carefully chosen and all the lighting elements are custom-made.

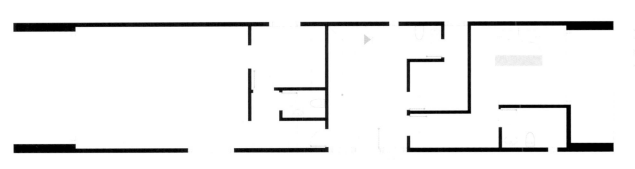

40 m² living
12.5 m² sleeping
9 m² kitchen
4.7 m² bathrooms

PENTHOUSE MUNICH GÄRTNERPLATZ

This house is a canvas for the imagination.
Let your mind run free!

Interior design | Gabriela Raible Innenarchitektur
Gross floor area | 117 m²
Address | Gärtnerplatz, Munich, Germany
Completion | 2009
Number of residents | 2 adults, 1 child

This is an ideal urban apartment for a businessman who required a retreat in the city and who likes to surround himself with art. The design is intended to reflect the desired separation of communication and privacy. The use of just a few colors leaves room for large, colorful artworks. The inner city roof terrace apartment stretches over two stories. The lower level houses the cooking and dining areas; one could say the 'active' communicative family rooms. A staircase leads to the floor above, where the living area is located. This features large windows and almost gives you the feeling of sitting outside. The living landscape features controllable furnishings and a hidden media technique, a tailor-made solution for maximal comfort and multifunctional use.

The surfaces of the built-in furnishings have been finished with a special matte varnishing technique.

30 m² living
22 m² sleeping
27 m² open-plan kitchen
12 m² bathrooms

This home was designed by Bob Hale, FAIA of Rios Clementi Hale Studios, for his multigeneration family. Three levels are defined on the exterior by the materials stucco, glass and aluminum. The stucco ground floor is built into the hillside. Glass encloses the middle and heart of the home, with living, dining, and kitchen areas that effortlessly flow together. Corrugated aluminum panels are water jet-cut with a pattern of the Hebrew word for love. The front yard is planted as a meadow and the rear yard is a grotto with a lap pool and spa.

BEIT HA-AHAVA – "HOUSE OF LOVE"

A declaration of a love of shadows and light.

Architect | Rios Clementi Hale Studios
Lightning design | E2 Lighting Design
Interior design | Rios Clementi Hale Studios
Gross floor area | 515 m²
Address | Los Angeles, CA, USA
Completion | 2012
Number of residents | 4 adults

The "House of Love" is so-called due to a screen of corrugated aluminum panels cut with a pattern of Hebrew letters spelling the word "ahava", meaning "love". The letters are arranged so that they can be read from both outside and inside.

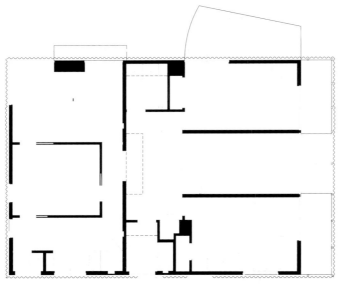

47 m² living
21 m² sleeping
31.5 m² kitchen
14.5 m² bathrooms
11.6 m² balcony

HIGH COUNTRY HOUSE

Neither spurs nor saddles ...
Simple elegance beats country style clichés.

Architect | Luigi Rosselli Architects
Interior design | Darryl Gordon Design
Landscape architect | William Dangar
Gross floor area | 364 m²
Address | Armidale, Australia
Completion | 2013
Number of residents | 2 adults

This hill top house is a concrete expression of Armidale's unique combination of rural life and culture. The clients seamlessly combine their flourishing agricultural business with their white collar occupations. The house is adapted to suit the sloping site; the volumes either project out over the hill, offering uninterrupted views of the stunning surroundings, or are embedded into the slope. Inside, the design functions as a canvas for the clients' collection of art and indigenous artefacts collected in Africa and Asia.

82 m² living
59 m² sleeping
29 m² kitchen
12 m² bathrooms
10 m² entrance

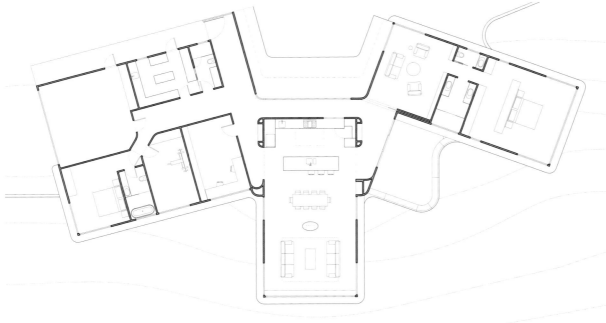

DW-HOUSE

Much more than just black and white, this house
juxtaposes colonial architecture with Asian esthetics.

Architect | Ong&Ong
Gross floor area | 757 m²
Address | Singapore, Singapore
Completion | 2011

The key reference point for DW-House is the archetypal colonial black and white bungalow; a culturally distinctive element in the architectural continuum of Singapore. The intention was to reinterpret the said monochromatic icon whilst not compromising on modern comforts. DW-House is a testament to the marrying of spatial sensitivity and stylistics, Western sensibilities with Asian esthetics, and the tradition of the black and white with contemporary architecture. The house seamlessly brings together seemingly polarized elements under a framework that is governed by achieving equilibrium and contrast, contextualized for a city that is itself extremely diverse.

43.36 m² living
99.9 m² sleeping
25.8 m² kitchen
50.43 m² bathrooms

95

The reinterpretation of tropical architecture reverberates throughout this design as seen in the classic white wood louvers that run along the second floor of the main house, promoting ventilation while acting as a distinctive style element, juxtaposing the black in true colonial bungalow fashion.

This house is located in a green district not far from the city center, but is still protected by its topography and lush greenery. The original landscape, typical of Austin, has been preserved to a great extent. The architects' immediate response to this exceptional landscape was to try to preserve the ancient elements by highlighting some of them: the trees, the garden, and the cave. The band of windows on the second floor enables all the household members to enjoy spectacular views of the surrounding landscape.

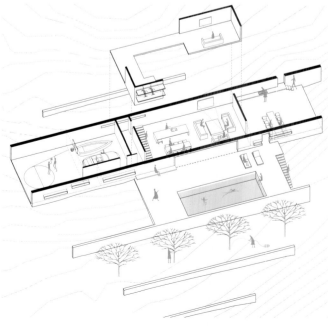

95 m² living
113 m² sleeping
29 m² bathrooms
31 m² study and gym
52 m² garage

GREEN HOUSE IN AUSTIN

Atmospheric conditions collide with changing
lighting conditions and spatial experience.

Architect | Jadric Architektur
Interior design | Jadric Architektur
Co-architect | Erik Gonzalez
Gross floor area | 320 m²
Address | The Trail of the Madrones, Austin, TX, USA
Completion | 2013
Number of residents | 2 adults, 2 children

The spatial arrangement of this house was carefully thought out. The north-south axis comprises a series of indoor and outdoor spaces that align themselves with a terraced slope to the south. The east-west axis is aligned with the movement of the sun.

BUKIT GAMBIR

Living the highlife! This tower offers stunning views of both the jungle and the ocean.

Architect | Spark
Interior design | Spark
Gross floor area | 75,000 m²
Address | Georgetown, Penang, Malaysia
Completion | 2017
Number of residents | 800–1,000

These two residential towers sit at the base Bukit Gambir, a lush tropical mountain located at the heart of Penang Island in the Indian Ocean off the western coast of Malaysia. The geometry and composition of the towers is inspired by the surrounding land and seascapes mediating between the steeply rising verdant mountain and the flowing currents of the Malacca Straits. The western tower is closer to the mountain, climbing to 49 stories, it will be the tallest on the island, offering spectacular ocean views from the upper levels of its eastern elevation whilst the western façade looks towards the jungle covered mountain. The lower tower rises to 27 stories, where the sculpted fin geometry steps back from the primary elevation creating a layered sky-garden sculpted from the upper floor plates.

The two towers are generated by the extrusion of a simple and efficient elliptical floor plate, whilst the façade is brought to life with the addition of a waveform fin at each level. The varying profile of the ledges is inspired by the ocean currents of the Malacca straits that separate the island from peninsula Malaysia.

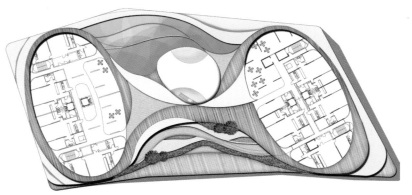

71.8 m² living (tower A, unit 8)
71.2 m² sleeping
19.9 m² bathrooms
5.4 m² lobby

This former commercial space has been converted into a loft apartment. The space is a wealth of contrasts, some areas are clad with light wooden panels while other areas, such as the kitchen, are more industrial in appearance. The kitchen units are clad with stainless steel, giving them a shiny and futuristic look. In the master bedroom the bed and headboard are characterized by their elegant and simple design. A walk-in closet covered with anthracite gray laminate is reflected back on itself from the full-size mirror. The bedroom is oriented towards the garden, making the most of the view. The combination of wood cladding and white walls gives the bedroom and living space a large, open and welcoming appearance.

52 m² living
31 m² sleeping
25 m² kitchen
17 m² bathrooms
15 m² corridors

LOFT CONVERSION

Inside meets outside and present meets future in the whacky and wonderful design.

Architect | Egue y Seta
Interior design | Daniel Pérez, Felipe Arauj
Gross floor area | 200 m²
Address | Terrassa, Barcelona, Spain
Completion | 2013
Number of residents | 2 adults

VACATION HOME ON 'EASTER ISLAND'

This family doesn't need to take anything when they are stranded on an island; this house already has it all.

Architect | Zaigas Gailes birojs
Interior design | Zaigas Gailes birojs
Gross floor area | 503 m²
Address | Kaltene, Latvia
Completion | 2010
Number of residents | 2 adults, 4 children

One morning the architect's family set out on a daytrip along the Baltic sea shore and found an artificial stone island with ruins of a former fish factory pumping station, built in the 1980s and abandoned soon after its completion. This industrial architectural monument to the Soviet era has been converted into a vacation home for the architect's family. The project preserves the island's landscape and architectural features. The original red brick façade is covered with rusty corten steel plates and sliding shutters with perforated images of stone Moai. A new Nautilus bathhouse, resembling the turret of a submarine, has been added to the back of the main house.

62 m² living
80 m² sleeping
29 m² bathrooms
153 m² hallway
10 m² balcony

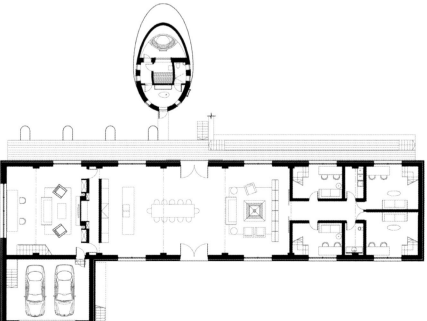

This project involved the renovation of a prefabricated house in Tokyo for a family with two children. Two stories in height, the house was built 25 years ago and the focus of the renovation work lay on the steel structure. The original design was divided into several rooms and hide the supporting frames. The architects have now revealed the steel frames, columns and braces and used them as important elements in the space. An opening was made through the second floor; this makes a visual connection through an expanded steel panel, from the new library for studying, reading and hobbies, to the living room, creating a feeling of unity between both floors.

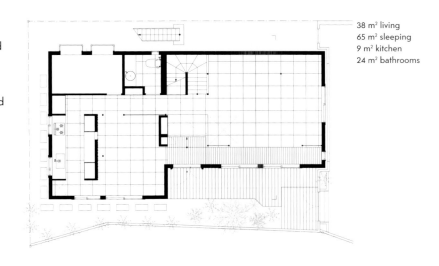

38 m² living
65 m² sleeping
9 m² kitchen
24 m² bathrooms

HOUSE IN SHIMOIGUSA

Explore a new way of thinking black and white!

Architect | Makoto Yamaguchi Design
Gross floor area | 154 m²
Address | Suginami-ku, Tokyo, Japan
Completion | 2012
Number of residents | 2 adults, 2 children

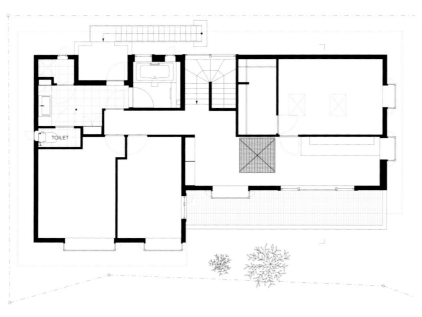

TOILET

A unique feature of this house is the exposure of the supporting steel frames. These give the property a strikingly industrial appearance. This feeling is reinforced by the open-plan layout and the uniform use of white and neutral tones.

LOFT APARTMENT

Bend it baby! This house has about as many straight lines as a plate of spaghetti.

Here, the walls move sinuously and curve gracefully through this loft apartment, housed in a former butter factory, West Melbourne. A sculptural staircase sits at the converging point in the space, twisting and soaring up towards a recreational roof terrace that overlooks the city of Melbourne. A monochrome palate of white on white with charcoal and black plays with the abundant natural light that is drawn in from the large north facing windows and ceiling void. An essentially open ground floor plan is defined by bending, wrapping walls that contain a bathroom, laundry and storage spaces. Sliding doors create the opportunity for expanding or containing, depending on how the ground floor is used, whether it be as a studio, bedroom or for entertaining.

Architect | Adrian Amore Architects
Interior design | Adrian Amore Architects
Gross floor area | 238 m²
Address | Melbourne, Australia
Completion | 2013
Number of residents | 1 adult

White is the shade of choice for this house. It doesn't need colorful accents because the dynamic curves and playfulness of the design are striking enough in themselves.

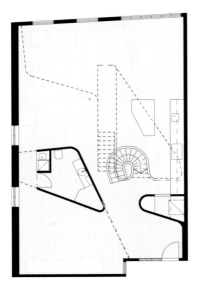

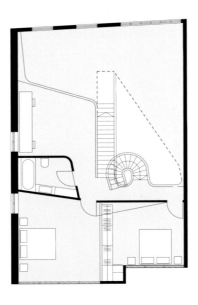

60 m² living
63 m² sleeping
15 m² kitchen
15 m² bathrooms
21 m² corridors

121

AGBARIA HOUSE

Sorry Mister Huntington. We prefer a multicultural mix to a clash of civilizations.

Architect | Ron Fleisher Architects
Interior design | Ron Fleisher Architects
Gross floor area | 380 m²
Address | Musmus village, Israel
Completion | 2010
Number of residents | 2 adults, 3 children

In a region where cultures usually clash, the house over the "wadi" (valley) in the village of Musmus is a multicultural experience. The plan reflects the client's will to maintain an independent Palestinian identity within the Israeli society. The main entrance to the property is more than 17 meters down the slope. Between the gate and main house a driveway curves in a reconstructed agricultural landscape. The slope was divided with traditional terraces made from local stone collected in the family's olive grove. The house shares a dialogue with the natural landscape using classical Muslim elements as well as contemporary technology.

The house design, with its perforated façade and the "liwan" – a long vaulted hall open to the outside – aid passive ventilation, keeping the house cool even in such a hot climate.

24 m² living
64 m² sleeping
42 m² kitchen
26 m² dining
20 m² bathrooms

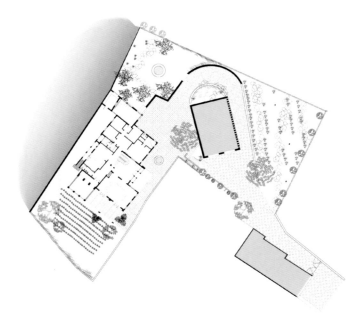

UNION SQUARE LOFT

No more art is needed...
This loft is a masterpiece in itself.

White, bright and tight, this four-bedroom urban duplex loft space houses a young family of four. The upper level is a communal space featuring a wall of windows facing south and east. The kitchen is tucked around the corner of the entry, allowing the dining and living spaces to breathe in sunlight and provide a wide open play space. The dining/living wall features a built-in storage space that cleverly hides the kids' toys. The bedrooms are located above the living area and are reached via a spiral staircase. The home was designed with family, play and art in mind. Much of the furniture is child-size. At the bottom of the stairs is an open play space that leads to a designated play/art room.

109 m² living
58 m² sleeping
15 m² bathrooms
10.5 m² office

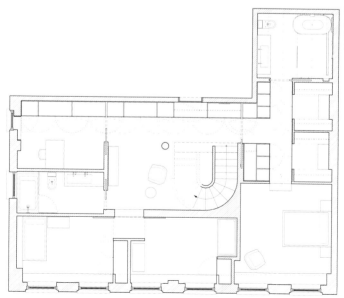

Architect | Resolution: 4 Architecture
Gross floor area | 278.7 m^2
Address | Lower 5th Avenue, Manhattan, New York, NY, USA
Completion | 2011
Number of residents | 2 adults, 2 children

Organization is important and the client was very hands-on throughout the design and construction process. The artwork in both the master bedroom and powder room, as well as some in the kids' rooms was created and composed by the client. She also designed the dining room table, selected the light fixtures, and all of the furniture.

COTTON STUDIO RESIDENCE

The perfect role model for a loft style à la Tribeca.
Everything is inspiring in this open living and working
space.

100 m² living
9 m² sleeping
15 m² kitchen
4 m² bathrooms

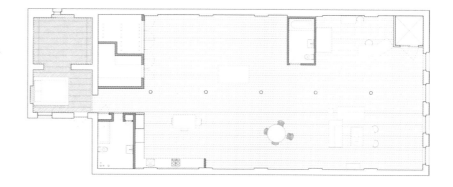

Architect | Tang Kawasaki Studio
Interior design | Tang Kawasaki Studio
Gross floor area | 268 m²
Address | 14 Harrison Street, 10013 NY, USA
Completion | 2011
Number of residents | 2 adults

Located in the TriBeCa neighborhood of New York, this live - and work loft was founded in one of the few buildings under the city's designation of "Artists-In-Residence" that was still fully occupied by genuine artists. The space was remodeled to house an artist and his partner and also serve as his primary studio for painting and sculpture. Living and working spaces were kept open to facilitate the artist's workflow, which is deeply inspired by food and thus a critical adjacency between the studio and the kitchen was maintained. Existing brick walls were sandblasted and treated with translucent layers of whitewash; the old plaster ceilings were stripped down to expose heavy timber joists and girders; reclaimed American oak floors were de-saturated to brighten the space.

From experimentation with titanium oxide based pigments in the hard oil floor compound, to the development of multi-layered hand finishing techniques and special tools, careful attention was paid to how light and texture would change over the course of the day.

MANDEVILLE CANYON RESIDENCE

The good old times are not yet over, they live on in this perfect mix of tradition and modernity.

Architect | Montalba Architects
Gross floor area | 204 m²
Address | 2767 Mandeville Canyon Road, Los Angeles, CA 90049, USA
Completion | 2011
Number of residents | 2 adults, 2 children

This single story 1950s California ranch-style home was badly in need of repair and updating, both inside and out. Montalba Architects found inspiration in the mostly covered-over details of the existing structure – a high exposed-beam ceiling in the living room and brick walls – and re-imagined these for an open, flowing series of rooms that a modern family could enjoy. The roofline was raised over the entire house and clerestories, skylights, and full-height glass doors were added to bring in additional natural light. A bright and reflective material palette is used throughout to visually expand the space and pay homage to the original mid-century character.

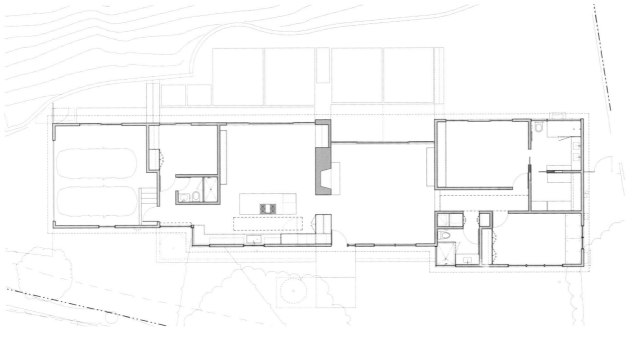

59 m² living
61 m² sleeping
18 m² kitchen
10 m² bathrooms

This interior design uses original furniture from the 1950s alongside modern elements to pay tribute to the origin of the house and underline its special character.

FEISTEINVEIEN

Not one, but one: This new extension is the yin to its yang.

Architect | Rever & Drage Architects
Gross floor area | 110 m²
Address | Feiseteinveien 24, Stavanger, Norway
Completion | 2013
Number of residents | 2 adults, 3 children

This extension to a single-family house in Stavanger was made to make room for a growing family in a city which has become increasingly developed over the last decades due to the economic boom related to the area's oil industry. The large extension to the north contains two small bedrooms on the upper floor, a living room at ground level, and a combined home-cinema-and-exercise room in the basement. The two bedrooms are reached by a winding staircase connected at the top by a glass platform-and-stairs leading to the roof terrace. The small extension to the south contains bathroom and main entrance.

A deep incision cut into this new building not only creates space for a small roof terrace; it also acts to visually separate the two volumes. Furthermore, the contrasting colors give the extension a new and independent character, making it an autonomous creation, rather than simply part of the existing house.

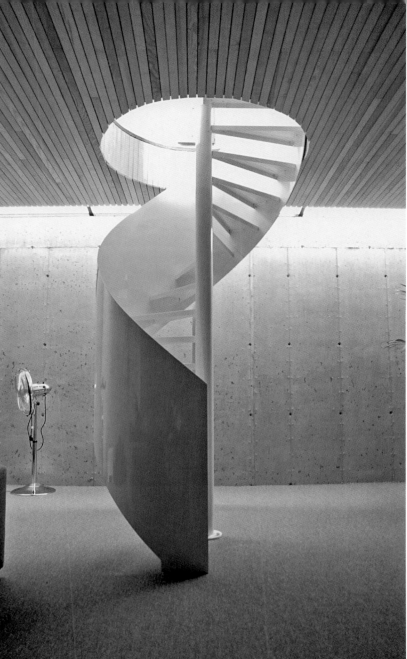

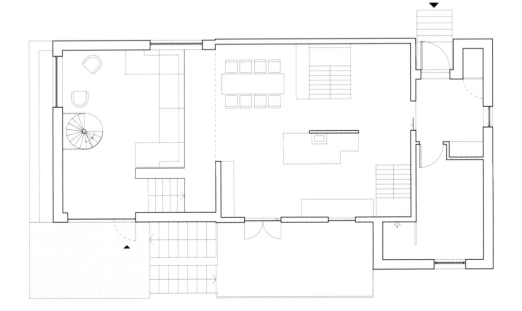

30 m² living
14 m² sleeping
35 m² home-cinema
11 m² storage

HOUSE FOR INSTALLATION

White walls, clear forms and lots of light:
This artists' residence is the perfect blank canvas
for inspiration.

Architect | Jun Murata / JAM
Interior design | Jun Murata / JAM
Gross floor area | 116.5 m²
Address | Kiyosu, Kashiwara, Osaka 5820006, Japan
Completion | 2014
Number of residents | 2 adults

This project involved the renovation of a house in Osaka, Japan. The house has been converted into a minimalist atelier and artists' residence. The dwelling is comprised of clear forms, minimalist detailing, and a thoughtful lighting design. The design seeks to promote a tranquil and open environment, appropriate to an artistic lifestyle. Beyond living spaces, the building houses studios, an office, and exhibition areas. The simple material palette includes white walls and ceilings, complemented by wood floors and furnishings. Simplicity, flexibility and the elegant use of light defines the living and working spaces, an abstract setting for calmness, meditation and creativity.

24.6 m² living and dining
7.5 m² kitchen
10.2 m² atelier

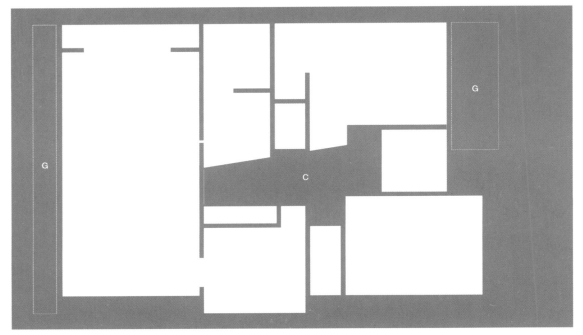

143

The primary room is characteristic of traditional Japanese architecture. The 'Toko' – a Japanese term generally referring to a built-in recessed space, in which items for artistic appreciation are displayed – unites the living and dining areas.

KILDEVEIEN VILLA

The perfect corner for a bookworm to sit by the fire, relax and enjoy.

40 m² living and office
31 m² dining
49 m² sleeping
20 m² kitchen
10 m² bathrooms
20 m² terrace

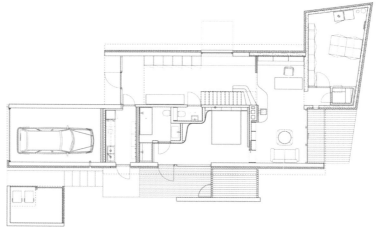

Architect | Lund+Slaatto Architects
Interior design | Lund+Slaatto Architects
Gross floor area | 220 m²
Address | Kildeveien 14, 0590 Oslo, Norway
Completion | 2009
Number of residents | 2 adults, 2 children

One enters this house via a welcoming entrance hall with a large window that overlooks the garden. The master bedroom on the ground floor is dominated by
a custom-built wall of oak, which conceals the bathroom. On the first floor the space
opens up to the living room and makes the most of views over the city and the
fjord. The fireplace has openings both into the kitchen and into the living room.
The material palette of the house is quite restrained. On the ground level the floor
is polished with white concrete, and the walls are rendered in pigmented plaster.
Upstairs the floor is oiled oak, while the walls as well as the ceiling are rendered
with the same natural white plaster as downstairs. All the doors are made in solid oak,
and feature elements such as the countertops in the kitchen and the fireplace
are made in grey marble.

The interior design is minimal and efficient, combining custom-designed furnishing solutions in oak with white concrete and rendered surfaces, giving the sequence of rooms a feeling of nature, light and strength. The consistent use of materials in the façade; using natural white mineral plaster and concrete stands in sharp contrast to the lush dark green vegetation around the house, transform the building into a sculptural form in the landscape.

This single-family house is located in the urban environment of the Bornheim quarter in Frankfurt. The design responds to the densely developed location, featuring an open-plan arrangement and making optimal use of natural light. A polygonal volume, covered with a homogenous anthracite gray cladding, stretches between two existing firewalls and houses the private areas and bedrooms. By contrast, the lower floor is completely glazed and becomes part of the outdoor garden area.

70 m² living
76 m² sleeping
40 m² kitchen
23 m² bathrooms

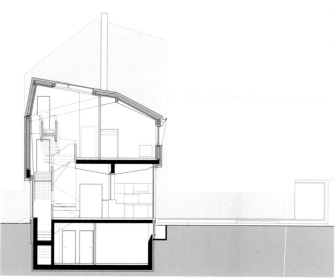

150

DINER – HOUSE

Like something straight out of a H. G. Escher drawing, this staircase almost appears to wind up into infinity.

Architect | LülingSauer Architecture
Gross floor area | 450 m²
Address | Frankfurt/Main, Germany
Completion | 2013
Number of residents | 2 adults, 2 children

A large 'diner' is located on the ground floor, opposite the open kitchen, and functions as a key communal area. The sculptural staircase spirals around this, leading up to the bedrooms above.

WESTRIDGE RESIDENCE

When an architect gets kissed by the Californian sun new spatial concepts erupt like a supernova.

Architect | Montalba Architects
Gross floor area | 442 m²
Address | 2120 Westridge Road, Los Angeles, CA 90049, USA
Completion | 2012
Number of residents | 2 adults, 1 child

Capturing 270-degree views of downtown Los Angeles and the Pacific Ocean, this massive foundation-up renovation and second-story addition floods the once-dark interior with natural light and creates indoor-outdoor environments throughout. Floor-to-ceiling windows combine with natural Ipe decks and rooftop rock gardens to extend view corridors and habitable areas at the south and west elevations. The newly added second story offers a separated haven for the extended family. Light-colored, beach-inspired materials such as white-washed oak floors, white stone, teak millwork, and ocean-toned glass tiles transform the home into a tranquil, airy Southern California retreat.

154

This entire color palette is dominated by warm, earthy beige tones that create a cozy atmosphere and draw extra attention to the wisely used colorful highlights of the furnishings.

55 m² living
152 m² sleeping ensuite
89 m² kitchen
18 m² bathrooms
21 m² foyer

DOMINION

Sit back and let yourself be taken back to the future.

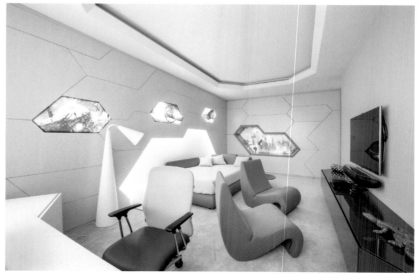

Architect | Geometrix Design
Gross floor area | 190 m²
Address | Moscow, Russia
Completion | 2013

This futuristic design is full of modern elements and state-of-the-art technology. The design is cool and clear, making good use of straight lines and angular, edgy elements. The natural tones used are complimented by a wealth of natural daylight, drawn in through the large windows. The home entertainment center almost looks like something out of a spaceship and is a dominating aspect in the living area. The interior design is an interesting mixture of soft brown and cream tones in the living areas and snappy black and white furnishings in the kitchen. The lighting has also been carefully designed to complement the desired atmosphere in each room. Bright white lights dominate in the kitchen and functional areas, while soft warm lights are used in the living and bedrooms.

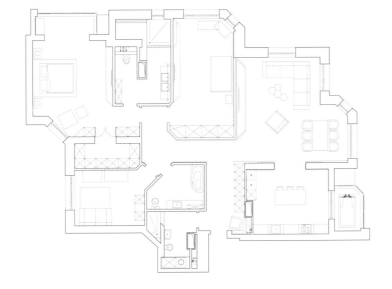

VILLA CP

Old and new have been fused together to create a
perfect symbiosis.

Villa CP is a restoration project undertaken on an old Catalonian farmhouse, and involved the creation of a 21st-century house inside an old stone structure. The existing
stonewalls have been largely rebuilt, with large openings that make the most of views
of the spectacular surroundings. The design is characterized by a mixture of old and
new. The old has been left visible with all its scars, while new materials such as corten
steel, wood and clay, were chosen for the beauty of their natural imperfections and
the way in which the traces left by time improve their appearance.

162

Architect | Zest Architecture
Interior design | Zest Architecture
Gross floor area | 440 m²
Address | Girona, Spain
Completion | 2013
Number of residents | 2 adults, 2 children

Large corten steel shutters provide shade on the south side and show the traces of raindrops on their surface when closed. An outside shower has doors perforated with blown up raindrop shapes, which throw a cascade of "sunshine drops" on the wall as the sun moves over the house.

35 m² living
71.9 m² sleeping
42.8 m² kitchen and dining
26.8 m² bathrooms
20.4 m² library

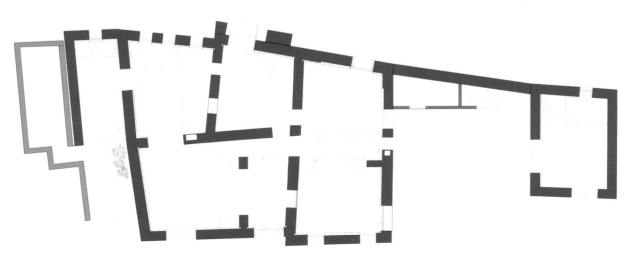

GLAMPING

Glamping it up in South Korea.

Architect | ArchiWorkshop.kr
Gross floor area | 50 m²
Address | Gyunggi-Do, South Korea
Completion | 2013

These modular units are inspired by the shape of a pebble, thus reinforcing the connection to their immediate environment. The units can be opened out at the front, so that users really get that camping feeling. Their arrangement also makes the most of the stunning views. The outer skin of the Glamping units comprises a PVDF (Polyvinylidenfluorid) membrane, which is completely waterproof and fire resistant. The double skin construction also offers some protection against the extreme Korean climate. The units have been grouped together, in a similar formation to that of tents on a campsite.

18 m² living
17 m² sleeping
3 m² kitchen
4 m² bathrooms

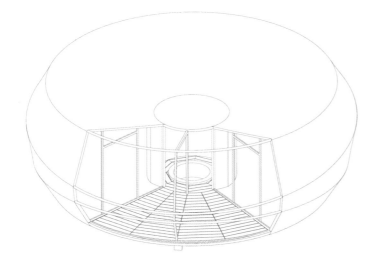

The word "Glamping" was introduced to South Korea over 10 years ago. This project focuses on putting the glamor back into camping and on reinvesting the word "Glamping" with its original intended meaning – the creation of a building or series of small buildings that truly get as close to nature as possible but offer more luxury than your average tent.

M-HOUSE

Take the plunge! This house has everything a family could wish for. Even a large swimming pool.

Architect | Ong&Ong
Gross floor area | 498 m²
Address | Singapore, Singapore
Completion | 2011

In keeping with the client's request, this home provides the ideal balance between the needs for both family and personal space. Sunlight enters from all sides of the house, providing illumination during the day whilst also keeping the interiors warm during cooler weather. The second level is also cantilevered, shading areas on the ground floor. The selection of materials used in various sections of the house was cost-effective, with an emphasis on high-grade quality without being excessively extravagant. A classic Modernist style was adopted through the use of fair-faced concrete and timber planks for the walls, as well as teak for some of the flooring and underside of the roof.

68.15 m² living
44.8 m² sleeping
36.3 m² kitchen
17.9 m² bathrooms

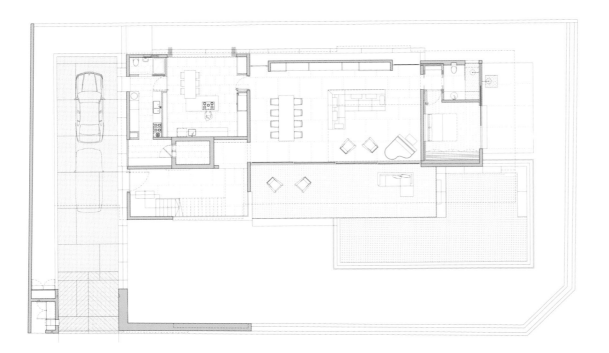

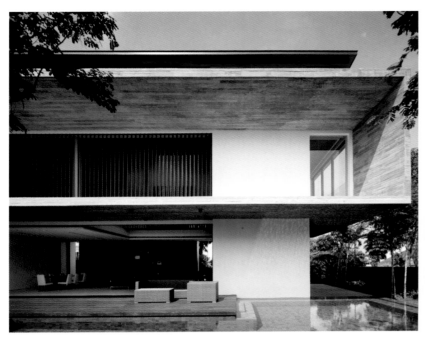

The concrete that covers the façade is unusual and looks almost like liquid stone. It adds a raw quality that is very fitting for this nature-inspired home.

RESIDENTIAL HOUSE IN LUDWIGSBURG

Light, white and bright – that's what happens when maritime style undergoes a reinterpretation in the German countryside.

Architect | Schneider I Architekten
Gross floor area | 548 m²
Address | Elisabeth-Kranz-Straße 17, 71640 Ludwigsburg, Germany
Completion | 2013
Number of residents | 2 adults, 2 children

This house is located on the edge of a residential area, directly adjacent to an open green space. Two building volumes have been arranged at right angles to each other. The main volume is oriented along the boundary of the plot from north to south. The side facing the neighbors is largely closed, while the garden side is fully glazed. The second volume is aligned along the south boundary. A second apartment is located on the lower level of the main building. The cellar, utility room and technical equipment are also all located here. The ground floor is characterized by the use of cream-colored natural stone. The loft is reserved for the parents' room and has been fitted with a carpet.

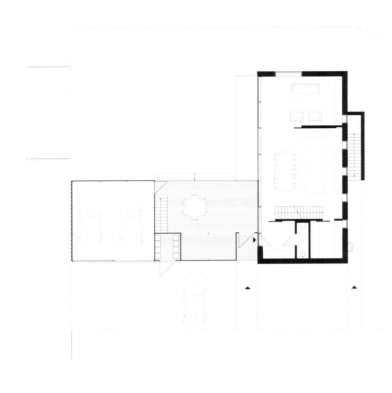

23 m² living
83 m² sleeping
38 m² kitchen
29 m² bathrooms
24 m² balcony

An open-plan cooking and dining area at the center of the ground floor forms the heart of the house.

P-901

Panorama views over the city, a luxury ensuite, an open-plan arrangement that almost seems to stretch into infinity – what more could you wish for?

Architect | Craft Arquitectos
Interior design | Craft Arquitectos
Co-architect | Michelle Cadena Chengue
Gross floor area | 395 m²
Address | Avenida Buganvilias 1000, Col. Bosques de las lomas, Mexico
Completion | 2012
Number of residents | 2 adults, 4 children

This design is based on the integration of various heights, materials and lighting. The striking lighting design gives each separate space a special character and emphasizes the modern appearance of the house as a whole. The introduction of cubes helps to define the spatial arrangement. One houses a sunken bath, separating it from the rest of the bedroom. A further cube in the living area acts as a functional unit, providing storage space but also dividing the dining from the living area without completely dividing one from the other.

151 m² living
85 m² sleeping
36 m² kitchen
75 m² bathrooms

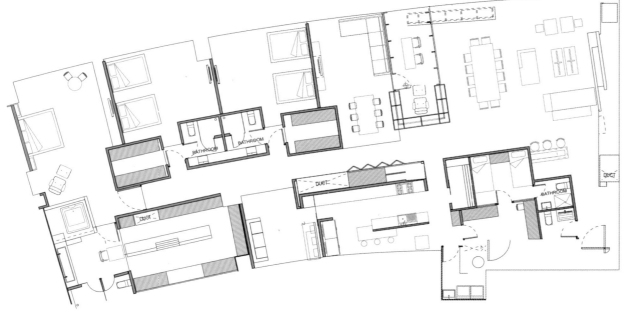

APARTMENT BUDAPEST

Out with the old and... in with the old. The striking materials used in the original design have been reinstated and newly interpreted.

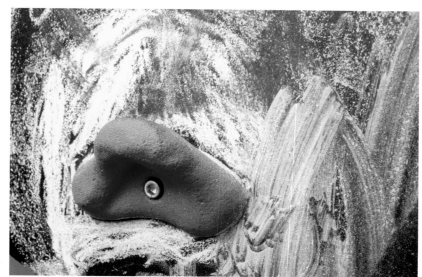

Architect | INpuls
Interior design | INpuls
Gross floor area | 125 m²
Address | Budapest, Hungary
Completion | 2014
Number of residents | 2 adults, 2 children

This apartment for a family of four is located in a peaceful rear courtyard in the heart of Budapest, not far from Andrássy utca and just a five-minute walk from the Danube. The apartment, a historical building with rooms three-and-a-half meters in height, has been completely renovated. Great importance was placed on maintaining then original materials and refitting them in the same style. The parquet flooring in the entire apartment, and the natural stone tiles were carefully taken out and the later reinstated. The rigid spatial division has been broken up to create large open rooms filled with natural daylight.

45.5 m² living
24.5 m² sleeping
12.5 m² kitchen
6.5 m² bathrooms
20.5 m² corridors

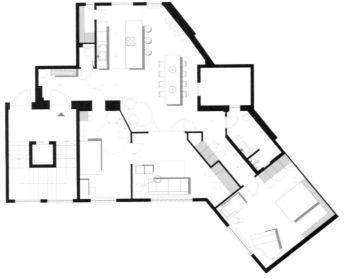

The combination of parquet flooring, mosaic tiles, vintage furnishings and modern objects create a light, comfortable and stylish atmosphere.

ART LOVERS

Snow White dressed up. A touch of color here
and there makes all the difference.

Interior design | Sophie Green Interior Architecture Brussels Munich
Gross floor area | 65 m²
Address | Rue des Mélèzes, Brussels, Belgium
Completion | 2012
Number of residents | 1–2 adults

This space was previously used as an office and the client demanded its complete
renovation and transformation into an apartment. The kitchen was renewed and a
new bathroom built. New openings were added and existing ones closed in order to
redefine the residential space. Existing niches were used for storage, thus allowing
optimal use of the available space. The height of the rooms and the absence of doors,
together with the chosen colors work together to create a 'loft' or 'gallery' atmosphere.
The walls, floors, ceilings are all white. In order to create a contrast, a dark material
was chosen for the work surface in the kitchen. The client's belongings add further
color contrast and dynamic accents.

Here, the white walls and surfaces function as a blank canvas for the client's colorful furnishings and art objects.

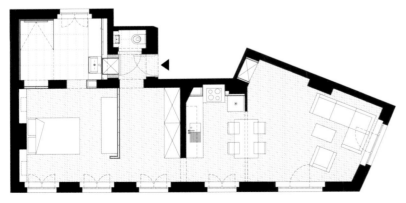

8.8 m² sleeping
17.9 m² kitchen
8.9 m² bathrooms

189

This interior design is a never-ending flood of contrasts – black and white, light and dark, sun and shade. Upon entering the bathroom or bedroom, one breaches the 'shadow side' stepping into a dark world of grays and dark tones. The rest of the apartment is bright and full of light. Several colored elements have also been integrated in order to break up the monotony of white furnishings; these help to dispel the sterile seriousness of the concept. Over time, as soon as the painted oak floor becomes slightly worn, the apartment will obtain vitality and become livelier.

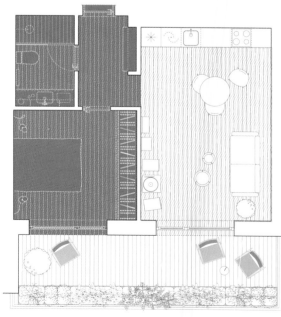

12.92 m² sleeping
23.66 m² kitchen and living
4.9 m² bathrooms
19.20 m² terrace

BW APARTMENT

A world of contrasts: Dark meets light and sun meets shade.

Architect | YCL
Interior design | YCL interior
Gross floor area | 46 m²
Address | Antakalnio Terasos, Žalakevičiaus Street, 10111 Vilnius, Lithuania
Completion | 2013
Number of residents | 2 adults

The color concept for the BW apartment is inspired by archaic traditions of living. The sleeping zone is a dark 'cave', without any distracting objects and suitable only for a calm and secure rest. The light side represents a 'hunting area' – light and vivid, and suitable space for receiving guests.

HOUSE 12.20

This clever design encourages not only thinking outside the box, but also thinking in the box.

38.16 m² open-plan space
3.28 m² bathrooms

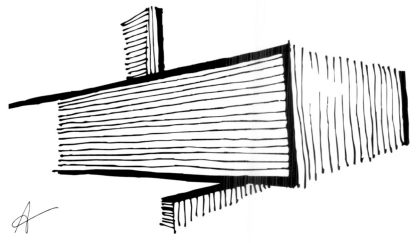

Architect | Alex Nogueira
Interior design | Alex Nogueira
Gross floor area | 45 m²
Address | Delcides Mariano street 1220, Rita Vieira, Campo Grande 79052-250, Brazil
Number of residents | 1 adult

The homogeneity of the internal space is an attempt at forming a dialogue with the external space, namely the green plane composed by the garden. Both the large sliding glass door and outside deck function as extensions of the internal space, making optimal use of the space available. The entire construction is raised slightly above the ground, giving it a more lightweight and dynamic appearance. The entire front of the house can be opened, which helps to passively cool the interior, creating a comfortable living environment in this hot climate. The clever use of space and the integration of white furnishings and natural tones make the space appear larger than it is.

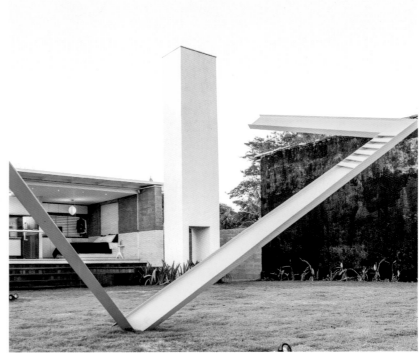

ARDMORE RESIDENCE

Green oasis in the urban jungle: This design brings the outside inside.

Architect | UNStudio
Interior design | Terry Hunziker Inc.
Gross floor area | 260 m²
Address | 7 Ardmore Park, Singapore, Singapore
Completion | 2013

The Ardmore Residence is an example of a new breed of residential towers. Located in a prime location close to the Orchard Road luxury shopping district, the Ardmore Residence enjoys expansive views of both the panoramic cityscape of Singapore City and the vast green areas of its immediate surroundings. The apartments in the Ardmore Residence embody the idea of a 'living landscape'. Functional spaces are redefined and extended into the living landscape concept, offering the occupants a flexible space. An indoor-outdoor living experience is achieved through the inclusion of large windows and double-height balconies in all of the residences.

The 'living landscape' concept is based on four specific details: the articulation of the façade, bay windows and double-height balconies; the adoption of the interior to accommodate two apartment types; the introduction of transparency and connectivity.

58 m² living
41 m² sleeping
14 m² kitchen
19 m² bathrooms

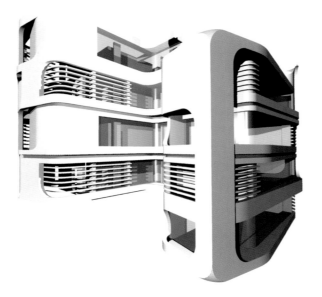

WOODEN FRAME HOUSE

Alternating between wooden façades and walls of glass, you'll find plenty of room to breathe.

Architect | a + samuel delmas
Gross floor area | 180 m²
Address | Sèvres, France
Completion | 2010
Number of residents | 2 adults, 2 children

Also known as the Filter House, this house is relatively closed towards the street. Frosted glass gives the residents privacy from the curious glances of passersby, while also allowing light to flow inside. Throughout the design, the play of transparent and closed spaces gives the house a dynamic character. The separate volumes each serve a different purpose, each offering a private space for the various family members. The choice of materials gives the house a more natural appearance, and with the tree raising from the terrace above, the house almost looks as if it has grown out of the ground where it stands.

The arrangement of the volumes creates a small green courtyard, this houses a tree and offers a quiet space to spend time and relax.

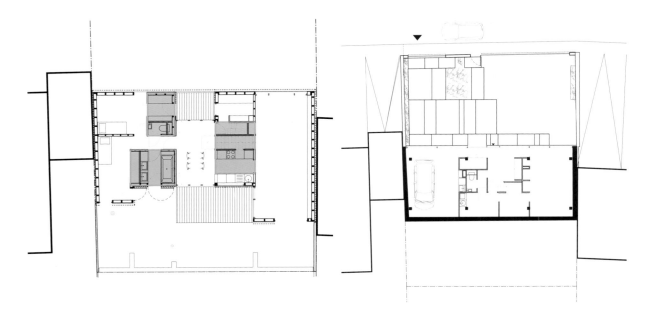

32 m² living
41 m² sleeping
18 m² kitchen
4.9 m² bathrooms
25 m² terrace

BOSQUE DA RIBEIRA
RESIDENCE

Here inside and outside mingle, flowing into each
other and coexisting in a perfect symbiosis.

127 m² living
97 m² sleeping
30 m² kitchen
23.5 m² bathrooms

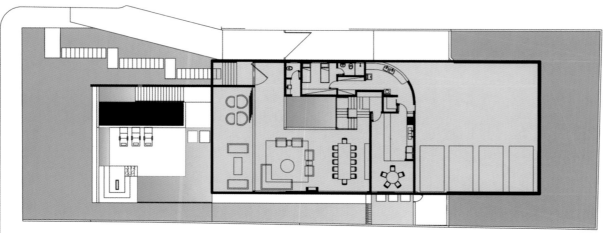

Architect | Anastasia Arquitetos
Interior design | Anastasia Arquitetos
Gross floor area | 590 m²
Address | Alameda dos Jacarandas, 244 Bosque da Ribeira Nova Lima, Brazil
Completion | 2013
Number of residents | 2 adults, 2 children

Bosque da Ribeira Residence is situated in a residential neighborhood, adjacent to an environmental reserve. The residence seeks to create a harmonious relationship with the environment. The landscaping designed complements its close relationship with the forest. The leisure area, swimming pool and terrace are designed to make the most of the surrounding landscape. A large covered balcony offers a space where residents can relax protected from the heat of the sun. A sauna and leisure areas are located at ground level, while the social areas can be found on the first floor and private areas on the upper level.

The upper floor has been hollowed out to create a covered balcony area. The integration of a large number of verandahs and terraces, open courtyards and large openings not only helps to draw daylight deep inside the house and aids passive ventilation, but also gives the house a strikingly open appearance, allowing all the separate spaces to flow together.

The floor plan of this house essentially corresponds with the original layout, although three important elements were added in the 1980s: a rustic wooden ceiling, a fire-place and a continuous built-in cupboard. The conceptual idea behind the renovation was primarily to expose the different layers. During the renovation work, two further original elements were brought to light: The black-white tiles in the kitchen and red-brown wooden flooring. Both of these elements were preserved; they were cleaned and conserved with wax. The original front door was also preserved. An important aspect of the design was to make the original elements visible, but also to emphasize the character of the new additions. For this reason, the kitchen has been fitted with shiny green kitchen units, thus creating a modern and colorful contrast to the warm tones of the wood and brick.

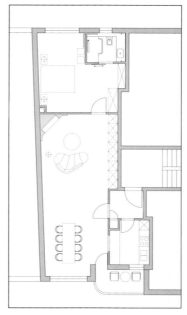

39.69 m² living
19.34 m² sleeping
5.97 m² kitchen
4.04 m² bathrooms
3.3 m² corridors

210

PRIVATE APARTMENT

Here, old and new work together in a perfect symbiosis; neither would be able to exist without the other.

Architect | kister scheithauer gross architekten und stadtplaner
Interior design | kister scheithauer gross architekten und stadtplaner
Gross floor area | 75 m²
Address | Hohenzollerdamm 35–38 / Mansfelder Straße 24, 10717 Berlin, Germany
Completion | 2014
Number of residents | 1–2 adults

Hans Scharoun built this building in 1930 and the apartments were designed for married couples without children.

THE SAN HOUSE

A house in the city with a pool and a rooftop terrace... and everything on a small plot. Let us play Jeannie.

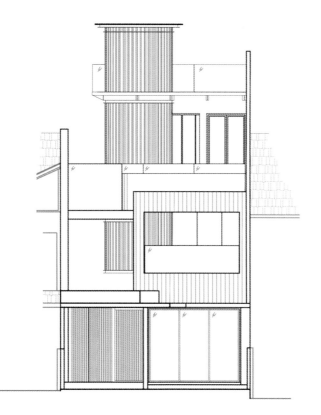

Although the plot size is rather small, just six by 22 meters, the brief from the client was for a private house to accommodate his three-generation family consisting of grandmother, father and mother, sister as well as the master of the house and his wife, and the live-in maid. The first story houses a separate living unit with three bedrooms, pantry and a living area for the grandmother, parents and sister with their own separate timber gate entrance. A large staircase from the main entrance leads upstairs to the second story where the main open-plan living and dining areas are located for the master of the house. The master bedroom is accessible via a spiral staircase from the front end of the living room terrace which also allows access to the pool for other members of the family or friends without going through the master bedroom.

Architect | Aamer Architects
Interior design | Aamer Architects
Gross floor area | 236 m²
Address | 34 Jalan Jintan, Singapore
Completion | 2011
Number of residents | 4 adults

215

71 m² living
73 m² sleeping
11 m² kitchen
20 m² bathrooms
22 m² corridors

The idea of 'boundless' space was the key forms this design. The private spaces, such as bedrooms, are separated, but the rest of communal rooms are connected and arranged as one fluent space. This open-plan arrangement starts at the entrance hall continues towards the living area space and kitchen. Throughout the interior many of the corners have been rounded off, which emphasizes the smooth and flowing character of the space. These 'softened' corners help to blur the boundaries of the walls, making them less defined. Even the staircase with its integrated fireplace and library climbs up around a rounded corner. The railing is made of a thin stainless steel net, so it is safe but smooth and transparent.

37.5 m² living
59.3 m² sleeping
12.55 m² bathrooms
9.5 m² gallery

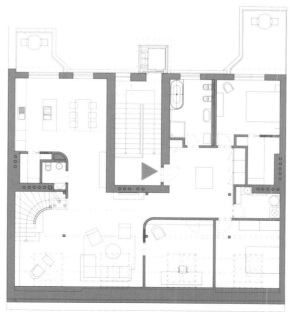

ROUNDED LOFT

Born free, as free as the wind blows... There are no
boundaries in this house and anything is possible.

Architect | a1architects
Interior design | a1architects
Gross floor area | 220 m²
Address | Prague, Czech Republic
Completion | 2011
Number of residents | 2 adults

Illuminated timber bookshelves highlight the fluent place and add storage space.

221

The experience of light in this house was a key focus of the design. During the day residents can enjoy a varied interplay of light and shadow, while at night the house almost looks like something from a James Bond movie.

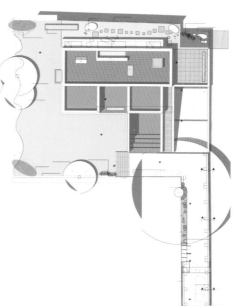

MODERN VILLA AS A CLASSIC

A chameleon among houses: The play of light
and shadow causes a dynamic and ever-changing
appearance.

Architect | Neugebauer Architekten
Gross floor area | 528 m²
Address | Höhenstraße 15a, 61476 Kronberg im Taunus, Germany
Completion | 2011
Number of residents | 2 adults, 2 children

The key focus of this project was to create a home for a young family with two children. The basement houses an additional apartment, a sauna and a multi-media room. Light is drawn into the space via a courtyard, which can also be used as an open-air cinema. The ground floor is organized into cooking, dining and living areas. A breakfast terrace is located above the double garage. The bedrooms are located on the upper floor. The largely transparent façade playfully responds to the alternation of solid and lightweight components, creating an interesting dialogue between inside and outside. An additional advantage of the design, is that part of the plot has not been built upon.

RESIDENTIAL HOUSE IN WALDENBUCH

Living on the border between the countryside and a residential estate means making the best of both worlds.

Architect | Schneider I Architekten
Gross floor area | 598 m²
Address | 71111 Waldenbuch, Germany
Completion | 2013
Number of residents | 2 adults, 1 child

This house is located on the edge of the residential area, where the urban area transitions into an open meadow landscape. The house comprises two volumes: The single-story flat-roofed building is positioned parallel to the slop of the site. The second volume has a saddle roof and is oriented towards the long side of the plot. The entrance is located on the ground floor and from their one accesses office, utility room, and guest bathroom. An open-plan cooking, living and dining area is located half a story above. The children's room is located on the next level, with the parents' room and a library above. A fitness room and sauna can be found in the basement.

66 m² living
57 m² sleeping
19 m² bathrooms
17 m² library
34 m² fitness

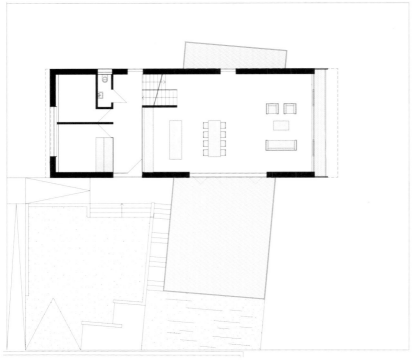

The open-plan cooking, living and dining area, and the parents' bedroom and library are all fully glazed and feature a balcony that offers views over the surrounding countryside.

229

SLM HOUSE

A big player in the neighborhood, and an
architectural composition of modern minimalism
and 1970s style.

Architect | archequipe
Gross floor area | 242 m²
Address | Solingen, Germany
Completion | 2013
Number of residents | 2 adults

Even before it was renovated and extended, SLM House was significantly larger than
the neighboring buildings. The addition of an additional story required an architectural solution that would both play down the size of the property, while also moving
away from the rather stocky appearance of the original house. The solution unites two
smaller volumes to form one house with two gables. Because the front of the house
is oriented towards the south, a verandah has been added on the ground floor. This
creates an optical buffer between the house and street, which protects the living areas
from excessive heat gain. The dark façade develops a dialogue with the area's more
traditional architecture.

231

The living space is arranged around a cube that incorporates a built-in closet, as well as a fireplace. Inside this central element, a staircase leads to the basement.

68 m² living
17 m² sleeping
41 m² kitchen
17 m² bathrooms
16 m² library

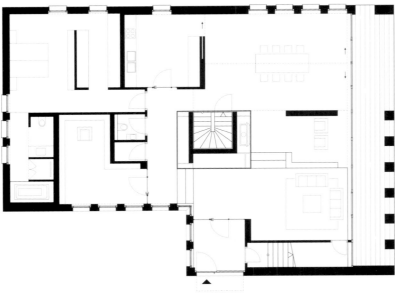

LIVING IN BRUNSWICK

Beauty is not a question of age:
The older the house the better it looks.

Architect | Nieberg Architect
Interior design | Nieberg Architect
Gross floor area | 467 m²
Address | Brunswick, Germany
Completion | 2013
Number of residents | 2 adults, 1 child

The client imagined a house that would be atmospheric and tranquil, with enough room for four people to live comfortably. After considering a number of different alternatives, the client decided upon an L-shaped open design oriented towards the nearby conservation area. The 450-square-meter single-family house is set back slightly from the street and has a modest and subtle character. The L-shaped volume creates a semi-enclosed courtyard that features a swimming pool. The architectural impression responds to the surrounding landscape, with the conservation area given more priority than the surrounding houses.

46 m² living
57.5 m² sleeping
26 m² dining
31 m² kitchen
24 m² bathrooms

A continuous motif throughout the entire design is the use of natural materials that develop a patina over time. This is inspired by Japanese Wabi-sabi – a Japanese world view that centers on the acceptance of imperfection and believes that naturalness is of greater importance than luxury.

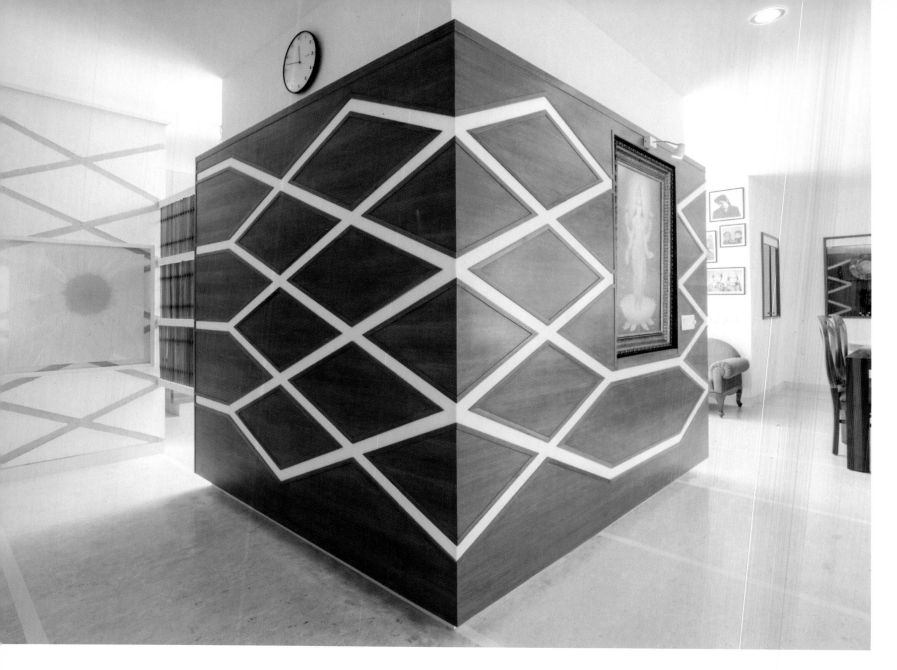

Originally intended as a minor restoration of a 1990s house in Bangalore, the Fragment House developed into a layered brief from the clients over the duration of two years. The existing building was transformed into a simple layout with a clear plan. Unnecessary areas were removed and utilized for storage. The external façade was not to be touched. Its daunting presence with large roofs and volumes were merely melted or accentuated to develop character for the front of the house. The altered volumes gave the house a new character. The new arrangement makes the space more accessible and draws light inside, creating a brighter and more modern interior.

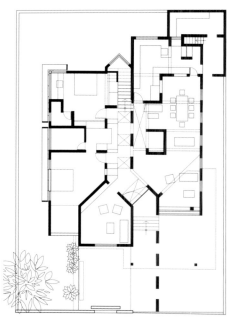

26 m² living
94 m² sleeping
16.5 m² dining
23 m² kitchen

FRAGMENT HOUSE

Out with the old and in with the new.

Architect | Gaurav Roy Choudhury Architects
Gross floor area | 334 m²
Address | Bangalore, India
Completion | 2012
Number of residents | 2 adults

The pooja room – a spiritual room for meditation – in the middle of the ground floor functions as a lamp, a sculpture and an anchor for the common spaces.

THE BOOMERANG HOUSE

Water, water everywhere... Enough to swim like a fish, bask like a shark or play like a dolphin.

Architect | Aamer Architects
Interior design | Aamer Architects
Gross floor area | 645 m²
Address | 13 Grove Grove, Sentosa Cove, Singapore
Completion | 2011
Number of residents | 2 adults

The site of this property is narrow and long. In order to maximize the view of the water, Aamer Architects designed the house to curve like a boomerang so that all the bedrooms could benefit. The geometry also allowed a 25-meter lap pool to be incorporated on one side at ground level. This lap pool continues as a water feature that wraps around the living and dining spaces. Inside, the design of the ground floor is fluid and continuous, so that, upon entry, one can see the waterfront straightaway. A linear timber deck that extends from the house to the pier further reinforces the connection to the waterfront. On the first floor the living and dining spaces are expressed as one fluid, continuous entity surrounded by water features and landscaping, while on the second floor, the spaces are divided into different bedrooms with ensuite bathrooms. On the third floor the architects have inserted a pavilion that serves as the home office or study for the clients, who work from home.

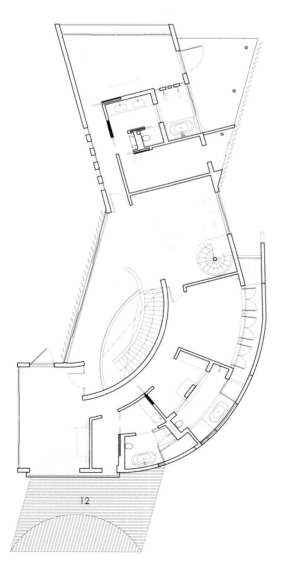

12

Water is a key part of this design. The house is not only connected to the nearby waterfront by a long pier, it is also surrounded by a pool.

195 m² living
110 m² sleeping
21 m² kitchen
53 m² bathrooms
25 m² corridors

BOUNDARY HOUSE

The sky is the limit when you live in a home that opens up to the surroundings and that allows you to glaze at the stars above.

Architect | Atelier Tekuto
Gross floor area | 100 m²
Address | Chiba prefecture, Japan
Completion | 2012
Number of residents | 2 adults, 1 child

This site is situated in an urban area between residential estates and farmland. The concept proposes a dramatic shift from economy-based to ecology-based lifestyle. The design was inspired by the idea of living under a tarp-like structure, where one can fully appreciate nature and move freely between inside and outside. The result was a maze-like composition where interior and exterior spaces are interwoven. A number of skylights were added, along with various plants that help to reinforce the interaction of nature and architecture. The exterior walls are finished with charred cedar wood, while the interior walls have been given a traditional wood finish. Both treatments have a similar character, once again reinforcing the connection between inside and outside.

18.9 m² living
18.7 m² sleeping
5.8 m² kitchen
7.5 m² bathrooms
14.7 m² corridors
12 m² courtyard
15 m² Japanese room

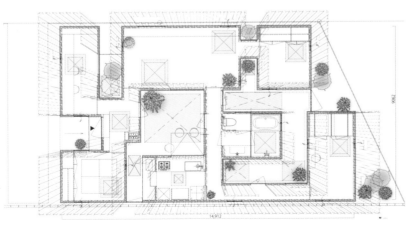

BARN AND DWELLING G

No milk today. But instead of cattle you'll find truly elegance.

Architect | Aeby Aumann Emery architectes
Gross floor area | 143 m²
Address | Tornalla 17, 1583 Villarepos, Switzerland
Completion | 2010
Number of residents | 2 adults

This barn and dwelling in Villarepos, Switzerland is perfectly positioned in a rural location of outstanding beauty. Situated on the outskirts of the village, the plot accommodates two different volumes: a family house and an outbuilding in the form of a cattle barn. Inside the dwelling, two rectangular volumes integrate the bedrooms, bathrooms and technical units, and delineate the living room and the kitchen, which open out with large windows that frame the surrounding environment. Six concrete blades support the dwelling, which almost appears to float above the fields. The location of this agricultural unit, its typology and the singularity of the materials used, offer a clear interpretation of the sustainable development and integration of a contemporary architecture in a rural environment.

Selected design classics and objects of art stage the corrugated fiber cement board.

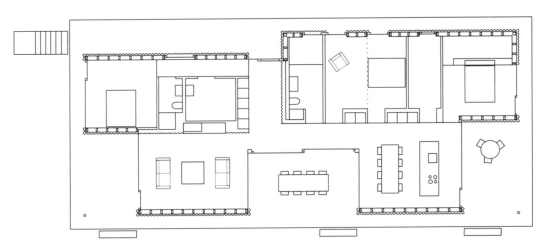

24 m² living
35 m² sleeping
33 m² kitchen
10 m² bathrooms
7 m² entrance area
15 m² studio

253

HOUSE S

Taking down the barriers in your house is like taking down those in your mind. Afterwards, anything is possible.

Architect | Alvisi Kirimoto + Partners
Interior design | Alvisi Kirimoto + Partners
Gross floor area | 140 m²
Address | Rome, Italy
Completion | 2012
Number of residents | 2 adults, 1 child

House S is a 140-square-meter apartment on the ground floor of a building built in the 1960s. The project involved renovation work that completely changed the original spatial arrangement. The clients love to cook and often cook for guests and friends. They wanted a design that would support this particular pastime. The new kitchen is a glass cube that faces the living room, accessible via sliding glass doors that are darkened by means of a shading system. The living room joins onto the terrace, which is equipped with a barbeque for outdoor cooking. A white bench runs around the perimeter of the living area. The entire design is strikingly modern and beautifully styled.

54 m² living
28 m² sleeping
14 m² kitchen
11 m² bathrooms
10 m² office

This whole house has been paved with stained oak planks that visually merge the space.

WANKA HOUSE

A jack-in-a-box of surprises; with this house one volume just appears to spring out of the other.

Architect | Estudio Galera
Interior design | Estudio Galera
Gross floor area | 470 m²
Address | 667 Avutarda, Cariló, Argentina
Completion | 2012
Number of residents | 2 adults, 2 children

Wanka House is a vacation home thought of as a playful space where family and friends can meet to relax. Located just 100 meters from the sea in Cariló – the design is inspired by the landscape and takes full advantage of the views. The living and dining rooms open out in an attempt to merge interior and exterior spaces. A white cantilevered box contains the bedrooms. Similar to a periscope, the box almost appears to float out from the main structure – covering the intimate terrace of the dining room and hanging over the grill area. The upper level of the house is dedicated to leisure activities.

259

This design comprises a series of box-like structures. The angular pool, square fire pit in the grill area, the steps, elongated balconies and the staggered volumes of the house itself all help to reinforce this.

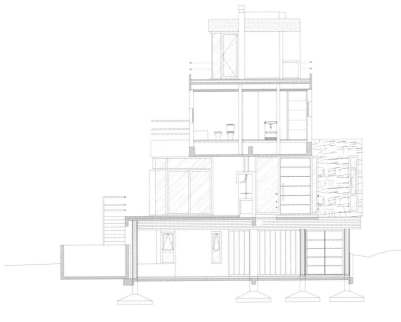

39.50 m² living
45 m² sleeping
19 m² kitchen
3 m² sauna

LIMANTOS

Taken literally, you are sitting in a glass house.

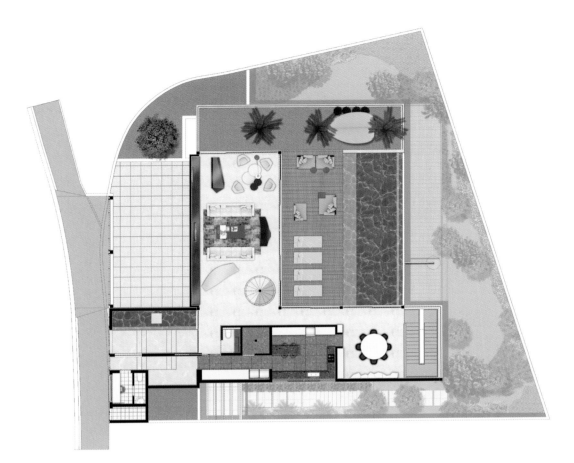

77 m² living
118 m² sleeping
41 m² kitchen and dining
58 m² home theater
36 m² kids' home theater

The lines of this house evoke the rationalist architecture of Mies van der Rohe. This project is all about simple geometry and the same integration dynamic, based on extensive use of glass. The prevailing theme that connects the two buildings is transparency. The idea of opening up the house to its surrounding space to better capture the light and create spectacular views for the occupants from different points of view. The spiral staircase provides access to the mezzanine, where the media room, fitness room and balcony are located. The lower floor houses the family area, and contains a playroom. Entrance to the master suite is via a wide hallway, which opens up to the two bathrooms, his and hers – and the walk-in closet.

Architect | Fernanda Marques Arquitetos Associados
Gross floor area | 830 m²
Address | São Paulo, Brazil
Completion | 2012
Number of residents | 2 adults, 2 children

263

The houses of Ludwig Mies van der Rohe (1886-1969) have a rational skeleton of steel beams that refer to the proportion used in the antiquity.

RESIDENTIAL HOUSE
NEAR FRANKFURT

Refashioning the old fashioned to create something new and exciting.

Architect | Architektur Sommerkamp
Gross floor area | 461 m²
Address | Hanau, Germany
Completion | 2013
Number of residents | 2 adults, 2 children

This single-story house was built in 1967 in the style of an American prairie house. The advantage of this is that the design seeks to combine indoor and outdoor spaces. However, the overall impression of the house was dark, old fashioned and somewhat unwelcoming. The redesign has given the urban villa a light and welcoming appearance. Inside the rooms simply radiate peace and quiet, inviting you to relax. For example, in the kitchen – which now includes a comfortable seating area – or in the living room. Here, exposed concrete harmonizes with the stone cladding on the chimney and the new curving bench near the fire. In the living areas, just a few natural materials form a harmonious, light and soft atmosphere. This creates a respectful environment for displaying the client's artwork.

84.9 m² living
66.9 m² sleeping
12.7 m² kitchen
31.25 m² bathrooms
15.6 m² library
21.6 m² entrance area

30-centimeter wide panels of Douglas fir have been used in the living room; the longest of which is an impressive 10 meters in length. The wide wood panels are extremely durable and eventually develop a patina, so embodying the ideal of sustainable design.

LIVING ON THE EDGE

I'll huff, and I'll puff and I... won't blow your house
down. This thatched house is as solid as a rock.

55 m² living
65 m² sleeping
33 m² kitchen
15 m² bathrooms

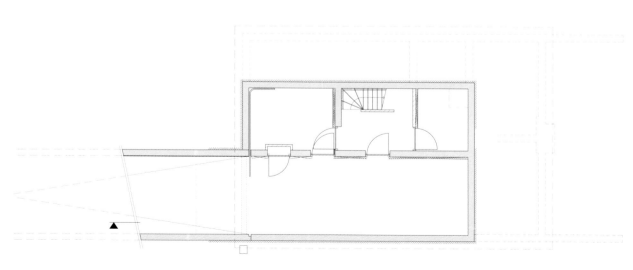

Architect | Arjen Reas
Gross floor area | 360 m²
Address | Zoetermeer, The Netherlands
Completion | 2010
Number of residents | 2 adults

This house was built for a private client, a businessman who wanted a quiet retreat where he could get away from city life. The architects wanted to create a house that would unite traditional ideals with contemporary house design. The fine texture of the hatch combined with smooth plaster surfaces creates the perfect blend of modern and contemporary. The main living space is a large open kitchen, this is connected to the garden by large glass sliding doors. The floor above houses the main bedroom, second bathroom and three other bedrooms.

One of the priorities while designing this house was to provide the residents with magnificent views of the landscape. Large windows built into the thatch draw light deep into the house and light up the space within, giving the interior a dynamic and welcoming character.

273

SOUTHERN HIGHLANDS HOUSE

Independent living in the heart of the Australian highlands.

Architect | Benn + Penna Architecture
Gross floor area | 154 m²
Address | Bullio, Australia
Completion | 2013
Number of residents | 2 adults

This design is for a new home-office pavilion, built alongside two existing pavilions on a remote rural property three hours drive south of Sydney. The new building is part of a set of three free-standing pavilions that each contain the separate functions of sleeping, living and working. The pavilions are loosely arranged at the base of a natural amphitheater formed by the towering sandstone cliffs of the Barragorang Valley. On approach, the pavilions appear like a cluster of farm buildings clad entirely in non-combustible metal sheeting and carefully designed to protect against fierce Australian bushfires.

274

A verandah wraps the entire perimeter of the building, appearing almost as if it has been carved out from the buildings mass. The depth of the verandah gradually alters depending on the aspect of the façade.

15 m² living
51 m² sleeping
10 m² kitchen
18 m² bathrooms
20 m² verandah

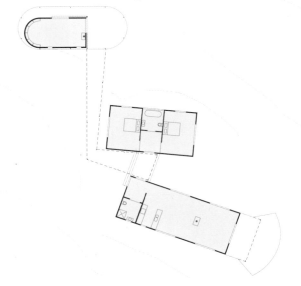

FRAMING THE SKY

In this house the sky really is the limit.

Architect | Atelier Tekuto
Gross floor area | 155 m²
Address | Tokyo, Japan
Completion | 2013
Number of residents | 2 adults, 1 child

This house is situated in an urban residential district in Aoyama, Tokyo. The program requested by the clients included a garage and bicycle parking space in the basement; a main entrance, bathroom and master bedroom on the ground floor; living and dining space with kitchen on the second floor; and children's room in the loft. The design is based on the concept of "framing the sky". The architects focused on the relationship between nature and people in the city and that the presence of skylights in most modern urban buildings has made the sky an extremely important part of everyday urban life. The volume of the house was determined by height restriction regulations.

38.72 m² living
10.98 m² sleeping
33 m² kitchen
10.24 m² bathrooms
16.2 m² loft

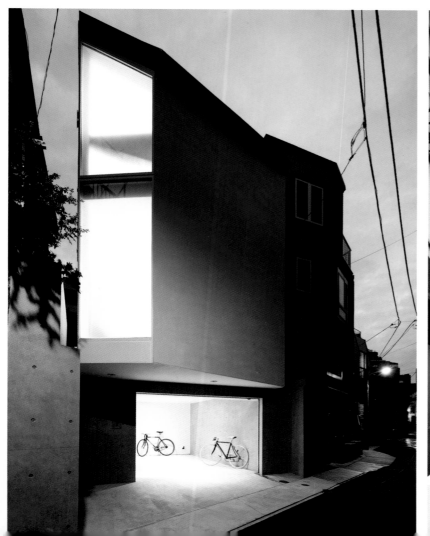

The large skylight is an integral part of this design. It draws light into the house and bathes those below it in sunlight. This large window makes the blue urban sky an important part of the experience of living in this house.

DM RESIDENCE

Up and down, around and around, this house draws you into the depth like a maze. The question is whether you will find your way out again, or if you would want to.

Architect | CUBYC architects
Gross floor area | 715 m²
Address | Flanders, Belgium
Completion | 2013
Number of residents | 2 adults

With this house, the architects have created a residence by developing a continuous play of coupled volumes, all interacting with each other. This 'play' gives the inhabitants different perspectives and spatial experiences. All living areas are visually connected with each other, and with the wooded area, but these subtle connections only reveal themselves in phases. The office has its own internal courtyard, the living room is connected to a walled pond, and the kitchen opens onto the covered terrace. The main terrace integrates a large swimming pool, clad with the same tiles used for the flooring and the façade. The house also includes a media room, fitness suit, a hamman and pool house, as well as a garage for four cars.

236 m² living
75 m² sleeping
50 m² kitchen
60 m² bathrooms
55 m² office

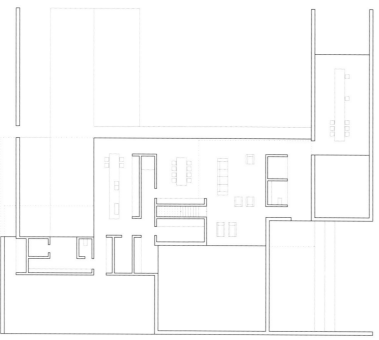

The façades are clad with ceramic tiles, arranged in vertical strips. These give the house a burst of white in the rather dark surroundings.

ATZ LIVING

Cube by cube. Stack it, shift it, link it and form
something new and unique.

Architect | Craft Arquitectos
Interior design | Craft Arquitectos
Co-architect | Michelle Cadena Chengue
Gross floor area | 140 m²
Address | Colonia Lomas Lindas, Atizapán de Zaragoza, Mexico
Completion | 2009
Number of residents | 2 adults, 2 children

The proposed concept was based on the intention of generating 15-meter-square modules. These modules can be adapted to suit individual needs and can even be extended if required. The property has been carefully adapted to suit the terrain. The modules are bound together by a structural frame of red steel. The design develops the idea of a continuous open-plan space, with all the interior spaces flowing into each other. The large windows allow an abundance of light inside, creating a bright and modern interior design.

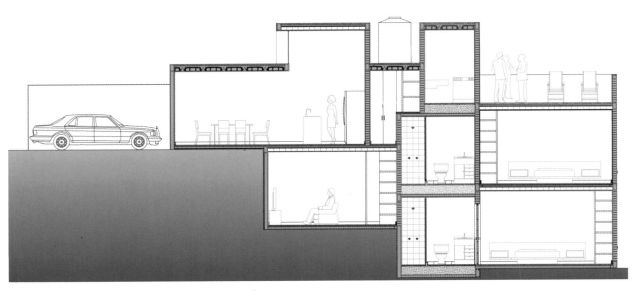

42 m² living
30 m² sleeping
9 m² kitchen
12 m² bathrooms

287

The stairs inside have been used to create diagonal lines in the glazed façade.

HOUSE NEAR THE RIVER REUSS

Here today, here to stay: this design can be easily
adopted to meet future requirements.

For this project, the client demanded a flexible design that would permit a sustainable
use of the site in the future. The basic shape of the building is derived from the site
of the plot. The two-story single-family house is modest in appearance and honors
the presence of the neighboring buildings. Towards the south, the house opens out
towards the Reuss river. The surrounding garden is also integrated into the design and
becomes part of the house. The sloping concrete walls follow the natural topography.
The solid upper floor houses the bedrooms and the entrance hall. The living spaces
can be found on the glazed lower floor. Inside, the warm oak panels create a striking
contrast to the glazed concrete walls.

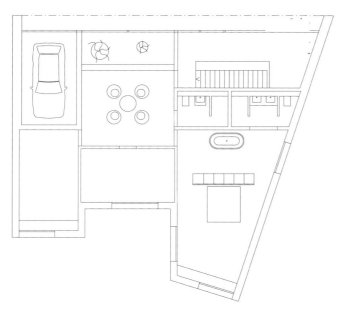 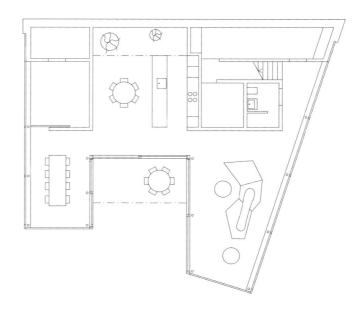

37.6 m² living
46.1 m² sleeping
37.5 m² kitchen
8.8 m² bathrooms
16.9 m² eating
17.2 m² entrée
23 m² library

Architect | dolmus Architekten
Gross floor area | 279 m²
Address | 6004 Lucerne, Switzerland
Completion | 2013
Number of residents | 2 adults, 2 children

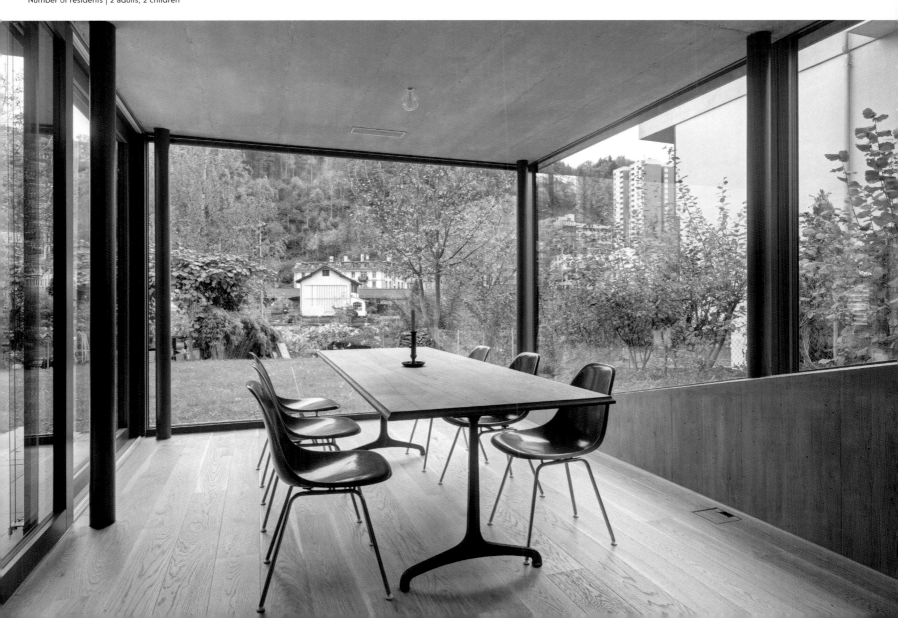

With just a few interventions this house can be separated into two apartments. The structure and pile system have also been designed to support an additional story if required in the future.

293

PENTHOUSE ON SAVIGNYSTRASSE

A gleaming white wonderland with each element perfectly complimenting the whole.

Architect | raab.schmale
Interior design | Schmidt Holzinger Innnenarchitekten
Gross floor area | 340.5 m²
Address | Frankfurt/Main, Germany
Completion | 2010
Number of residents | 2 adults

This apartment combines exclusivity and elegance. The tall cupboards in the kitchen develop into snow white, high gloss wall panels. The aquarium is integrated into a white volume and sits flush with the white panels above and below. This volume also functions as a clever storage element. The door leading to the utility room is barely recognizable as such, and the technical fittings belonging to the aquarium are hidden behind white lacquered fronts.

The matte surfaces of the wardrobes only reveal their finesse when they are opened. Inside, they are finished in light oak wood.

67 m² living
14.5 m² sleeping
54 m² kitchen and dining
23.5 m² bathrooms
19 m² balcony
15 m² dressing room
17 m² office
90 m² roof terrace

CASA VR TAPALPA

Rising like a stone fortress, this house presides over
the landscape.

243 m² living
118 m² sleeping
40 m² kitchen
38 m² bathrooms
120 m² corridors

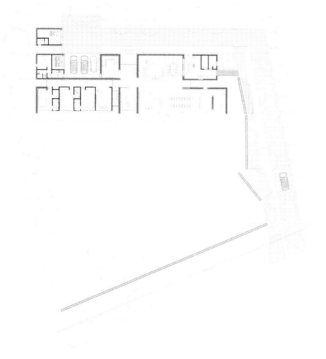

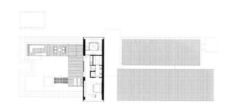

Architect | Elías Rizo Arquitectos
Gross floor area | 770 m²
Address | Tapalpa, Jalisco, Mexico
Completion | 2013
Number of residents | 2 adults, 2 children

Casa VR Tapalpa is an exercise in clarity and functionality. The program is arranged on four quadrants, which are defined by the intersection of two main circulation axes. Within this system, spaces are distributed according to privacy requirements and affinity. The design of the house was driven by the desire to allow it to connect with the outdoors and to converse with its regional context using a contemporary vocabulary. The building's front façade is fairly opaque and has few openings. At the back of the house windows allow daylight in and make the most of the views of a large lawn and the landscape beyond. The south-east quadrant contains three bedrooms, each fitted with its own bathroom, and a family room, the southwest quadrant houses the service spaces, a stairway and the garage. On the second level, the master suite spreads out across both quadrants and provides private access to a generous roof terrace.

A steel frame lifts the eaves to create an inward slope on the roof. This is complimented by the use of steel to accent various elements throughout the house, like the stair railings, the roof planter-parapet, and the frame at the open end of the second floor volume.

SU HOUSE

Great art deserves a great setting. No wonder this
house is a piece of Constructivism at its best!

Architect | Alexander Brenner Architekten
Interior design | Alexander Brenner Architekten
Gross floor area | 1,150 m²
Address | Stuttgart, Germany
Completion | 2012
Number of residents | 2 adults, 2 children

Located on a plot at the edge of a wood in a district characterized by its many villas in the south of Stuttgart, this villa was built for an art-lover and her family. The ground floor features a range of differentiated spatial situations that are not only suited to everyday family life, but also for hosting parties and special occasions. Skylights and raised ceilings create large rooms flooded with light. The design creates the perfect canvas for exhibiting the client's artworks but also creates intimate spaces for quiet retreat. The spa and pool area occupy most of the garden level, which opens out towards the garden. The private rooms are located on the upper floor and arranged around the gallery. The architecture, interior design, furnishings, lighting and garden were all designed and carried out by the architects.

69 m² living
36 m² sleeping
38 m² kitchen
24 m² master bathroom

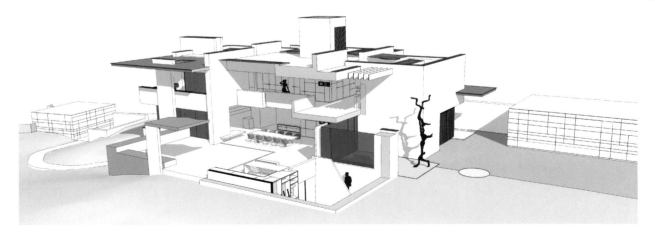

GOLD BAND ON BLACK

Pure gold: this treasure just screams quality.

Architect | fabi architekten
Gross floor area | 370 m²
Address | Flurstraße 7, 94405 Landau, Germany
Completion | 2011
Number of residents | 2 adults, 3 children

Approached from the south, this plot near the river Isar is in harmony with nature. Single-story volumes have been built facing the south in order to maximize the amount of sunlight reaching the open areas. The two-story volume towards the north-east is arranged to create a protective barrier around the pool and entrance court-yard. Living, cooking and dining areas are all housed in the single-story volume. The façades oriented towards the garden are glazed from floor to ceiling. A wellness area with a gym and sauna is located on the ground floor of the two-story volume, facing the garden and pool. The private rooms can be found on the upper floor. The exterior of the building is largely black.

This building was clad with RAL 9005 thanks to a new coating system (carbon fiber reinforcements and silicon carbide). 300 liters of black and 40 liters of metallic gold for the meandering band that runs over the volume.

42 m² living
50 m² sleeping
49 m² kitchen
15 m² bathrooms
67 m² fitness

68 Stapleton Hall Road is an urban development of two unique four-bedroom houses arranged symmetrically in a butterfly plan around a central axis on a constrained brownfield site in North London. The exterior draws inspiration from the local Victorian and Edwardian architecture but inside the spaces are generous light filled volumes. Designed collaboratively by architect-led developer Solidspace and Stephen Taylor Architects, the two houses are designed around a split section form, which offsets floors by half a story. Rooms are arranged around a double-height space and connected by an open stair, allowing daily activities – eat, live, work – to take place with differing levels of openness and privacy.

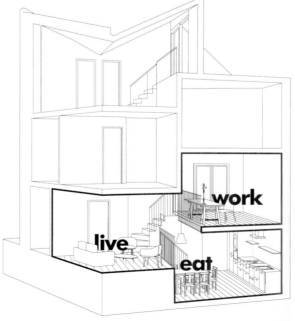

68 STAPLETON HALL ROAD

Just a touch of color won't just change the room,
it will change your life.

Developer architect | Solidspace Developments
Architect | Stephen Taylor Architects
Gross floor area | 146 m²
Address | 68 Stapleton Hall Road, London N4 2QA, United Kingdom
Completion | 2014
Number of residents | 2 adults, 2 children

An elegant enclosed handmade stair of Douglas fir leads to bedrooms on the upper floors and above them to a 'green' zone, where the parents can escape into their own suite of bedroom, bathroom, study and roof terrace.

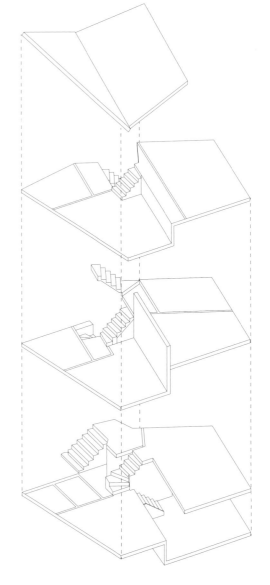

RESIDENTIAL HOUSE NEAR WESTPARK

This house might be at the end of the line, but it's not the end of the line for design.

Architect | Architekturbüro Stefan Krötsch
Gross floor area | 360 m²
Address | Specklinplatz 38, 81377 Munich, Germany
Completion | 2013
Number of residents | 2 adults

This house is situated at the end of a row of houses in Munich. The new building is wheelchair-accessible and replaces a dilapidated building from 1948. The L-shaped design forms the end of the row to the north, while the south façade offers views over the neighboring garden. The stairs in the center connect two separate areas that vary considerably from each other in terms of their spatial design. On one side, smaller rooms such as bedrooms, secondary rooms, and a lift are spread across three floors; while on the other side, the living areas boast an open-plan arrangement and form an open room continuum that develops across all three levels. Despite its east orientation, natural light enters from the west and is drawn deep into the building.

315

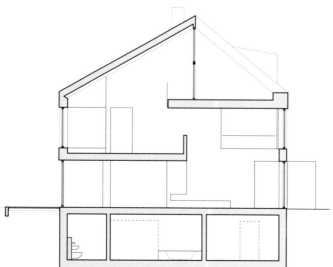

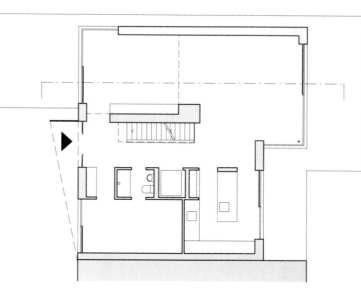

57 m² living
20 m² sleeping
20 m² kitchen
15 m² bathrooms
31 m² gallery
28 m² studio

BLACK ON WHITE

Perched like a nest in the treetops, this house offers perfect bird's-eye views of the surroundings.

Architect | fabi architekten
Gross floor area | 100 m²
Address | Schönbergerstraße 46, 93173 Wenzenbach, Germany
Completion | 2012
Number of residents | 1 adult

This house comprises two basic volumes; a black saddle roof that is rotated and cantilevers out over the white flat-roof box beneath. This arrangement reduced the intervention into the sloping topography. The two volumes are open towards the nearby forest. The building presides over the site with a certain air of tranquility and self-confidence. The house is set into the sloping site and visitors enter the house area via a high entrance hall. A room for working, thinking, talking, eating, partying, and relaxing is located on the upper floor. At night, the house offers space for retreating and sleeping.

65 m² living
19 m² sleeping
8 m² bathrooms

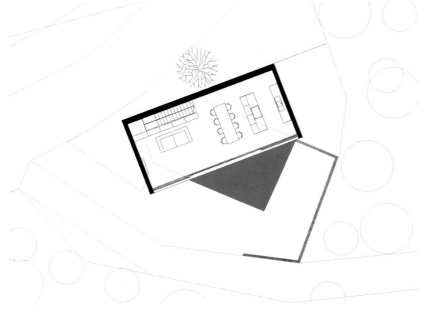

TOWNHOUSE ON WIELANDSTRASSE

This house is so understated it is almost an exaggeration.

Architect | Jo. Franzke Architekten
Gross floor area | 355 m²
Address | Wielandstraße 3, 60318 Frankfurt/Main, Germany
Completion | 2010
Number of residents | 2 adults

Located in an area characterized by buildings built in the Wilhelminian style, the Hunzinger townhouse closes the last remaining gap on Wielandstraße, Frankfurt. The size of the plot demanded a tailor-made solution for the five-story building. Luxurious living areas are located on each floor, allowing the client and other residents to enjoy 'living vertically'. A terrace is located on the roof of the house, which offers views of Frankfurt's skyline. The building presents a deliberately plain and elegant face to the street. The precise natural stone façade gives the property a monolithic appearance, subtly underlined by the color of the joins between the stones, which have been carefully plastered to make then the same color as the brick.

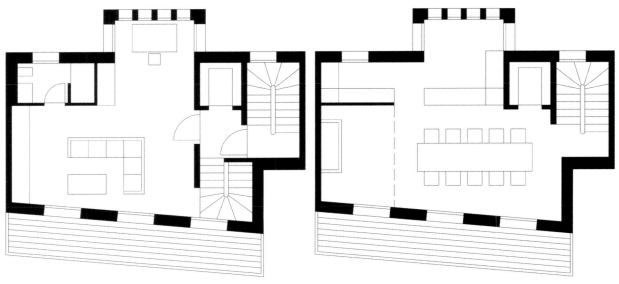

130 m² living
32 m² sleeping
70 m² kitchen
27 m² bathrooms
50 m² corridors

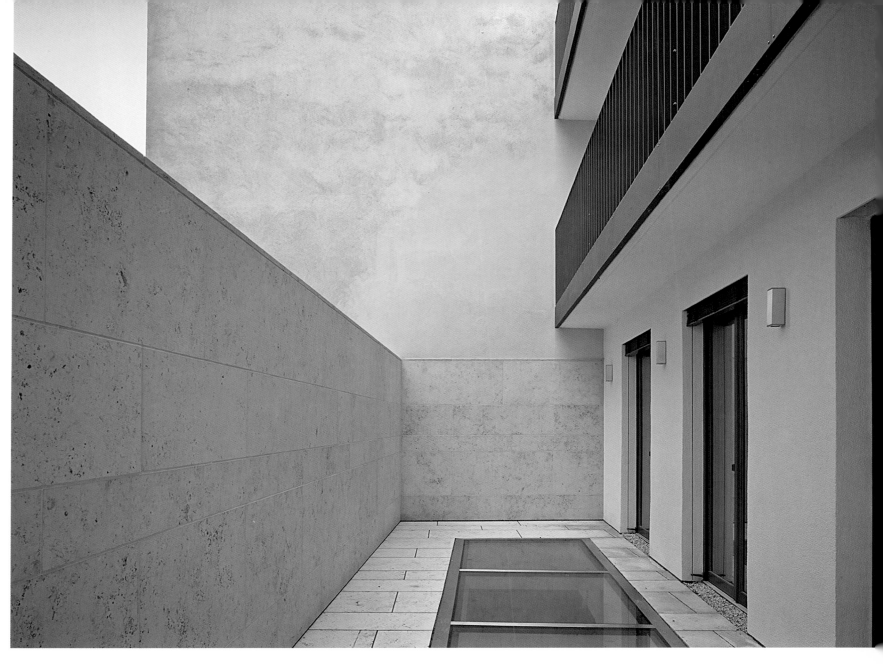

High rectangular windows and a stone oriel in the center dominate the solid façade. It respects the surrounding, fitting neatly into the streetscape and responding to the height and style of the neighboring buildings.

325

53.32° N / 9.59° E

We shape our environment, and our environment shapes us.

Architect | Behnisch Architekten
Interior design | KBNK Architekten
Gross floor area | 160 m²
Address | Hübenerstraße 1, 20457 Hamburg, Germany
Completion | 2012

This apartment is located on the 15th floor of a residential high-rise in Hamburg's Hafencity. The architects were faced with the task of creating a design that responded to the character of the tower as a whole. The spatial organization is characterized by flowing lines and a series of spaces that merge seamlessly with each other to form a coherent whole – from the entrance, through the living and dining areas and into the bedrooms. Numerous elements are integrated into the curving walls. This serves as a common element that gives the design a sense of unity. Cupboards, shelves, wardrobes and the kitchen are all integrated as built-in elements, which make optimal use of the surfaces without compromising the appearance of the space as a whole.

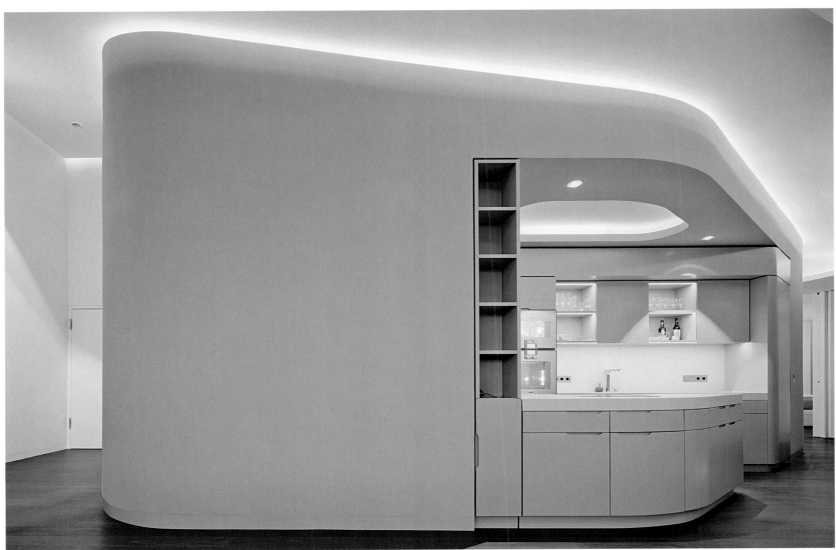

The lighting is carefully designed to perfectly complement the character of the apartment. Recesses cut into the ceiling are gently illuminated and pick up on the curving lines of the walls, while the volume housing the kitchen is emphasized by lighting above.

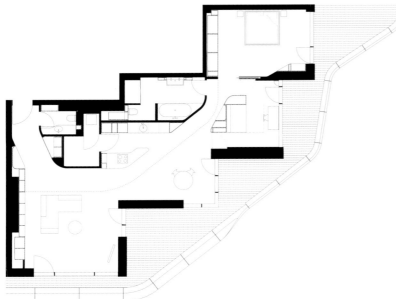

NEUFERT HOUSE

Warm light shines though the cold metal façade –
proof that it is what's inside that really counts.

23.4 m² living
32.8 m² sleeping
33.9 m² kitchen
16.3 m² bathrooms
13.2 m² corridors

Architect | Gatermann + Schossig Architekten Generalplaner
Gross floor area | 170 m²
Address | Cologne, Germany
Completion | 2013
Number of residents | 2 adults

This new house is located next to a listed property, X1 built by Peter Neufert in 1959. Intended for his widow, the house is barrier-free and also features an optional self-contained apartment. The single-story cube was built on the existing tennis court. Two smaller volumes have been 'cut' from the main volume and placed on the roof. This arrangement creates two higher rooms that offer views across the park and draw light into the house. The homogenous metal façade contrasts the colorful X1 House next door.

This house meets the low-energy house requirements thanks to the incorporation of a number of environmentally friendly energy features, such as concrete core activation, an air-water heat pump and controlled ventilation.

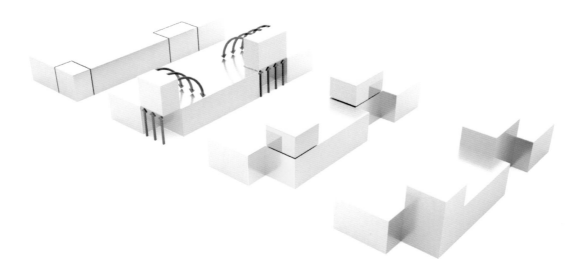

NASU TEPEE

A tepee in the woods; you can't get much closer to nature than this.

Architect | Hiroshi Nakamura & NAP Co.
Interior design | Hiroshi Nakamura & NAP Co.
Gross floor area | 148 m²
Address | Nasu, Tochigi Prefecture, Japan
Completion | 2013

The key idea behind this design was to use high ceilings to let direct sunlight into the house. This is of extreme importance as the site is located is in the midst of dense woods. In order to eliminate unnecessary space, the architects cut down the upper space diagonally, based on the way people move. The new form matches the tree branches that spread out radially and the ceiling descends like a tent that mingles with the trees. It is similar to primitive spaces seen in the houses of the Jomon People (Ancient Japanese) and Native Americans. A fire, a light or a table are set in the middle to initiate conversation as the family gather at the center of the house.

335

The clients are a married couple who enjoy organic farming on the weekends. Their wish was to preserve as much of the environment as possible. Interior details like the sliding door with dried flowers emphasize this contact with nature.

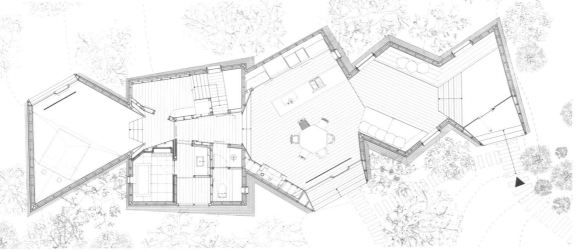

Depending on the function of the space and the desired atmosphere, colors, materials and furnishings have been carefully selected to create a relaxed and elegant living space that has also a hint of Asia. For the client, it was extremely important to have an interior architecture that was elegant yet natural modern and contemporary. The timelessness of the design forms a comfortable and relaxing background for this large and spirited family. The large living and dining area is arranged around the large fireplace an connected to the kitchen. A highlight in the kitchen is the large functional breakfast bar, from where one has excellent views over the lake. The contrast between classic stylish elements with warm, natural materials, such as a matte stone floor, dark parquet and sand-colored walls give this design its striking dynamism.

73 m² living
113 m² sleeping
28 m² kitchen
50 m² bathrooms

HOUSE BY THE LAKE

This house is so close to the lake you can almost touch the water just by leaning out of the window.

Interior design | Gabriela Raible Innenarchitektur
Gross floor area | 650 m²
Address | Fünfseenland, Bavaria, Germany
Completion | 2012
Number of residents | 2 adults, 3 children

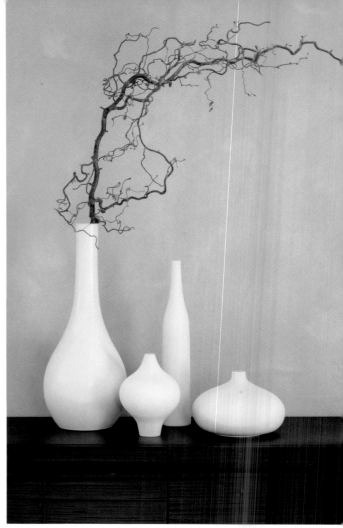

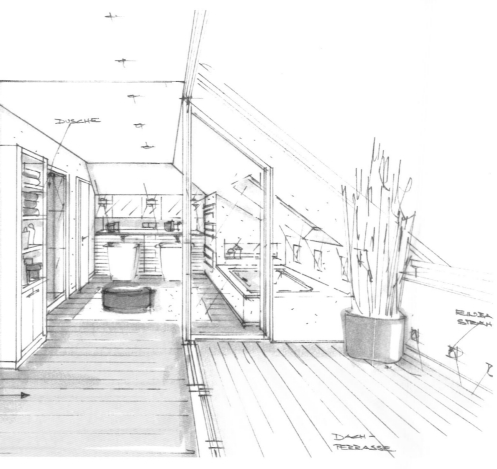

Classic villa elegance is mixed with modern and Asian elements.

BELLEVUE 50

A careful touch here and a tweak there and what was once old now becomes new.

Architect | KBNK Architekten
Interior design | KBNK Architekten
Gross floor area | 1,280 m²
Address | Bellevue 50, 22301 Hamburg, Germany
Completion | 2011

This historical villa was built in 1900 and is an example of a freestanding villa with views of the river. Within the framework of comprehensive renovation work, the building was renovated from the ground up and an underground garage was added on the street side. The existing façade was restored to its original grandeur, while the plastered façade with its ornamentation and real-wood window frames corresponds to the historical façades on the neighboring buildings. The extension in the garden is a harmonious addition to the existing building, but does not attempt to hide the fact that is a new addition. The modern façade features large windows that offer stunning views over the garden and also draw an abundance of light and fresh air inside.

Top-quality materials, such as chalked panels of smoked oak and natural stone give the interior a touch of timeless elegance.

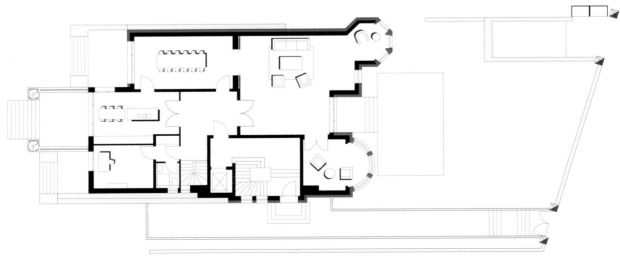

345

CASA CAMAR

The perfect house – as long as there are no termites around...

Architect | Jachen Könz
Co-architect | Ludovica Molo
Gross floor area | 184 m² each
Address | Via Collina d'Oro 44, 6926 Montagnola, Switzerland
Completion | 2008
Number of residents | 8 adults, 8 children

Casa Camar is an apartment building comprising four residential units that develop in a staggered arrangement over four levels. The shape and position of the building were defined by the plot boundaries. Wall elements facing the street modulate a row of concave rooms that all feature large windows and openings in order to effectively mediate between interior and exterior. The apartments are all organized over two levels with the bedrooms below and kitchen and living area above. The staggered arrangement makes it possible for more light to be drawn inside via the roof terrace to the south-west. The apartments are oriented towards the north, which makes optimal use of the views over the landscape.

52 m² living
54 m² sleeping
24 m² kitchen
13 m² bathrooms
24 m² corridors

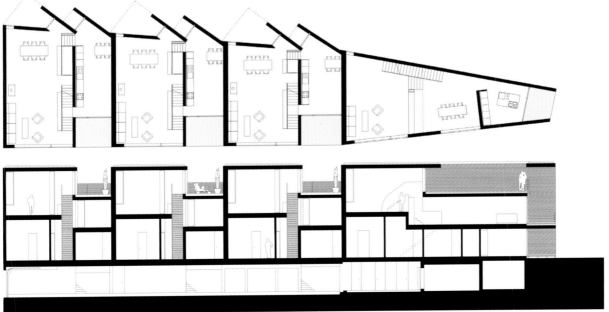

347

BRAHLER RESIDENCE

This house is so alive it almost looks like it might walk off at any moment.

The architecture of this house merges landscape and building surfaces, articulating the envelope of the addition while configuring the site into differentiated formal and informal spaces. A densely wooded perimeter provides privacy from the compact suburban neighborhood. The client wished to maintain the quaint cottage style of the existing century-old shake clad structure, while enhancing it with open interior spaces filled with natural light. A new master suite, gallery and indoor or outdoor entertaining spaces supplement the existing program. Inside, one encounters an environment characterized by layered views that create subtle connections to the exterior.

Architect | robert maschke Architects
Gross floor area | 115 m²
Address | Bay Village, OH 44140, USA
Completion | 2011
Number of residents | 2 adults, 2 children

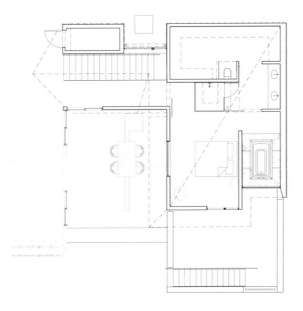

29.1 m² living
20.9 m² sleeping
19.5 m² bathrooms
11.5 m² gallery

GLOBE OUTLET VILLA

Mirror, mirror on the wall, who is the fairest of them all? Everywhere you look you can see reflecting elements, glass, crystals, illuminated ceiling.

Interior design | In-between Design Office
Developers | Hunan Richly Field Outlets Real Estate
Gross floor area | 270 m²
Address | No.558 LeiFeng Road, Wangcheng District, Changsha, Hunan, China
Completion | 2013
Number of residents | 4 adults, 1 child

In-between Design Office was invited to design a show house project for the Globe Outlet Villa to demonstrate contemporary villa lifestyle in China. The key concept was the pursuit of a harmonious ambience that would support and enhance family life. There are four floors in the villa and each floor has its distinctive highlights. Room composition is a critical design focus in this house. The overall layout is designed to balance individual privacy and family life. Each space has been given its own identity by the combination of materials, colors, artworks, texture and light.

355

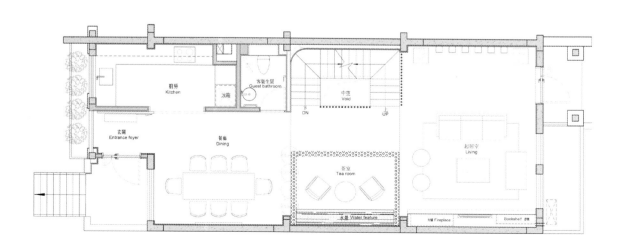

23 m² living
8 m² kitchen
14 m² dining
12 m² tearoom
3 m² entrance foyer

One of the key elements of the design is the 'in-between' idea of space and functional flexibility. The tearoom on the ground floor acts as a transitional space that connects the dining and living room via open pivot vintage mirror finished partitions.

357

MINTZ RESIDENCE

This house takes the guise of a shape-shifter, or maybe it is really your mind that is changing...

Architect | robert maschke Architects
Gross floor area | 402 m2
Address | 1305 West Fifty-Fourth Street, Cleveland, OH 44102, USA
Completion | 2009
Number of residents | 2 adults

Designed for a couple, one of whom is a photographer, the program called for spaces to live, work, and play. These were distributed on four levels due to a limited footprint and a desire to take advantage of the spectacular views afforded by the site. The Mintz Residence is an urban villa located on Cleveland's near west side. Uninterrupted views of Lake Erie and Cleveland's downtown and industrial flats, as well as the site's proximity to a busy vehicular thoroughfare, keep the project connected to its environment. Instead of a monolithic geometry, the multiple shapes suggest a subtle integration into the dramatically sloping hillside. As the volumes stack and overlap, the resulting interstitial spaces form a series of terraces and cantilevers which shelter exterior space.

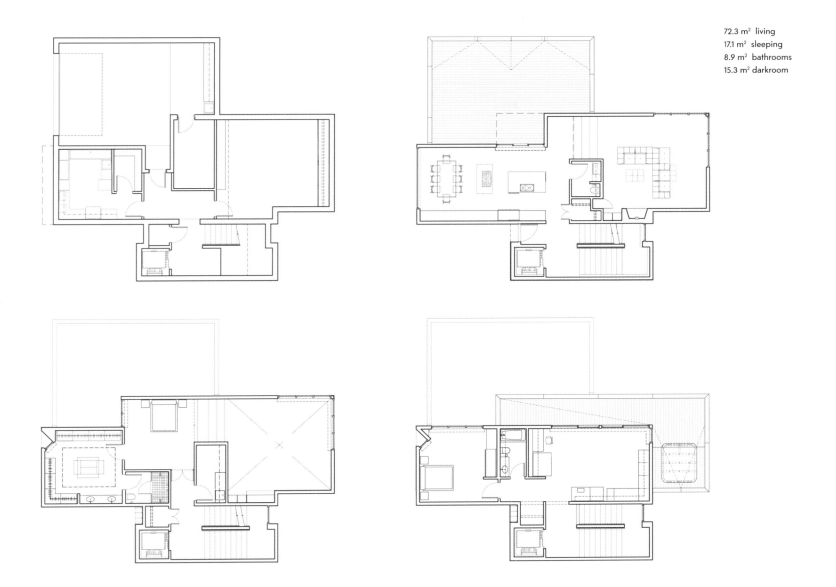

72.3 m² living
17.1 m² sleeping
8.9 m² bathrooms
15.3 m² darkroom

The architecture of the Mintz Residence is articulated as a series of minimal and discrete volumes which continually stack and shift, both in plan and in section, generating the building's massing. More than a compositional device, these formal manipulations take advantage of the singular opportunities and constraints of the site.

PARKVIEW

In this design tranquility is the true luxury.

Interior design | Joey Ho Design
Gross floor area | 168 m²
Address | Hong Kong, China
Completion | 2011
Number of residents | 3 adults

This apartment is home to two generations of a family who have lived there for more than a decade. As the family grows, the ownership of the home gradually changed hands from the parents to their daughter. Hence the need to rejuvenate the home, and inject it with new energy. The space has also been re-thought and re-configured to accommodate the different lifestyle needs of the daughter and the parents, all under the same roof. The mountain view is a key focus of the design. Both the living and dining areas open up to the extensive view of the mountais. In the master bed-room, the designer consciously explored the potential of the existing windows, using them to frame the views. The unobstructed view connects the interior with the great outdoors, making you feel at one with nature.

24.99 m² living
32.79 m² sleeping
13.38 m² kitchen
7.43 m² corridors

363

Curved elements are employed to further dissolve the boundary between different functional spaces. In the dining area, a curved feature wall was carved and wrapped by curtain-like fabrics, adding a soft touch to an otherwise rigid structure.

AM OBEREN BERG HOUSE

Wow! What a view. This house really is a feast
for the eyes.

Architect | Alexander Brenner Architekten
Interior design | Alexander Brenner Architekten
Gross floor area | 1,530 m²
Address | Stuttgart, Germany
Completion | 2007
Number of residents | 2 adults, 3 children

Located on a sloping site above the vineyards, this large multiple-generation house
offers unrivaled views over the city of Stuttgart. The design not only offers the residents the necessary comfort and protection expected of a family home, it also fulfills
the client's desire for transparency and develops a dialogue with the surrounding
nature and landscape. When one enters the house from the north-east, the two-story
entrance hall opens out towards the garden at the rear of the house, from where one
can enjoy views over the pool to the valley beyond and then further to the sloping terrain opposite. The environmentally friendly aspects of the design, such as the use of
renewable energy, also characterize the design of the outdoor areas. Half of the plot
has been left undeveloped.

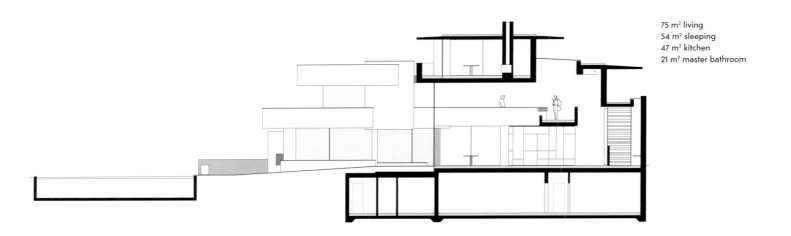

75 m² living
54 m² sleeping
47 m² kitchen
21 m² master bathroom

The clients wanted to create the perfect family home, located on Costa Rica's Pacific coast and overlooking the ocean. The site presented a challenge because the terrain is very steep and only the upper section of the site offered views of the ocean. This gave the architects the opportunity to develop a tailor-made solution that would respond to the site and the specific conditions. The architects took the decision to raise the house, allowing vegetation to grow beneath it and having as little impact on the area as possible.

20 m² sleeping
16 m² open-plan kitchen
8 m² bathrooms

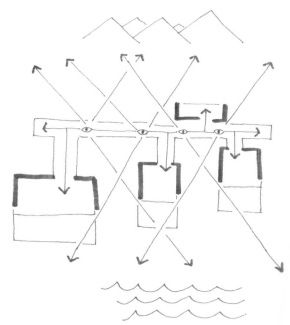

CASA FLOTANTA

Hang loose. Everything in this design simply demands that you watch the ocean and just breathe.

Architect | Benjamin Garcia Saxe Architecture
Gross floor area | 300 m² (3 buildings)
Address | Puntarenas, Costa Rica
Completion | 2013
Number of residents | 2 adults, 2 children

The use of wood throughout the building helps it to blend in with its surroundings, while a bathroom facing the hillside and an outdoor bamboo shower bring the occupants closer to nature.

ZOG HOUSE

The Queen wouldn't be amused: a white stranger among Victorian neighbors.

Architect | Groves Natcheva
Developer architect | Solidspace Developments
Gross floor area | 175 m²
Address | 1A Donaldson Road, London NW6 6NA, United Kingdom
Completion | 2010
Number of residents | 2 adults, 3 children

Built on a restricted brownfield plot at the end of a terrace in North West London, Zog House is a new build three-bedroom family house designed around the 'Solidspace' split section form. The split section, which offsets the floors by half a story, provides generous, flexible and connected spaces that suit modern day lifestyles. Designed in collaboration with Groves Natcheva, Zog House responds sculpturally and geometrically to the neighboring properties so as to avoid overlooking or loss of light. The clever arrangement allows each of the family members to find and inhabit their own space within the building but still feel connected to one another.

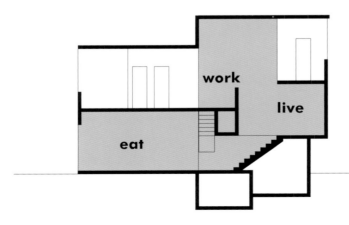

The rough look of the walls of exposed concrete with grey-green patina is supported by vintage factory lights and mid-century furniture.

HOUSE NEAR THE SEA

¡Viva España! The fan-like spatial arrangement radiates luxury, tranquility and a peaceful affinity with the Mediterranean Sea on every level.

Architect | Keggenhoff I Partner
Interior design | Keggenhoff I Partner
Gross floor area | 1,320 m²
Address | Mallorca, Spain
Completion | 2013

There is no place on earth that offers more diversity than living by the sea. The changing power of the water, its appearance and its ability to reflect the surrounding landscape inspired the creation of a special place in which to relax. The ground floor has a flowing spatial arrangement and houses an office area, indoor and outdoor kitchen and a spa area oriented towards the pool. The private areas are located on the upper floor, while technical equipment and services can be found in the basement. The outdoor areas pick up on imaginary lines that radiate from the house and are staggered to suit the sloping site.

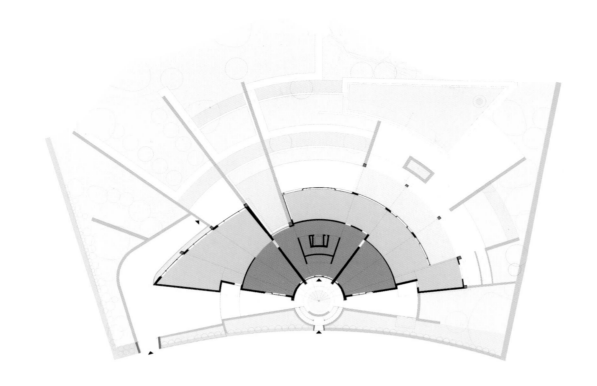

This is a house for young couple in typical residential area in Tokyo. The site is surrounded by neighboring houses on all sides, which made it challenging for the architects to devise a solution that would enable them to open the house up to draw light in but still provide privacy. Inside, the rooms comprise a series of beams, each rotated by 11.25 degrees. This produces a strong, rational structure reminiscent of a tree. The main space is divided to four different spaces characterized by this a large tree-like column. All spaces have different height and width compositions. The dining and living areas are well lit, while the bedrooms are dimly lit, giving them a more cozy and private atmosphere.

66.76 m² living
2.43 m² loft

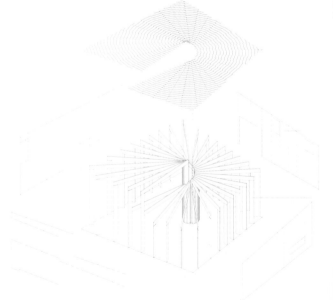

TREE HOUSE

This house is a real family tree, with rooms to meet
each individual need.

Architect | Mount Fuji Architects Studio
Interior design | Mount Fuji Architects Studio
Gross floor area | 80 m²
Address | Tokyo, Japan
Completion | 2009
Number of residents | 2 adults

The use of a solid column to spatially divide rooms is a typical Japanese architectural solution. This timber column and roof design create an interesting interior landscape, and create the impression of being under the spreading branches of a large tree.

385

QUEBRADA HOUSE

A tree house is a free house, located high up in the branches with views usually only enjoyed by birds and animals.

Architect | UNarquitectura
Gross floor area | 40 m²
Address | Curacaví, Santiago Metropolitan Region, Chile
Completion | 2013
Number of residents | 2 adults

The client requested a tree house design, so this house was therefore located near the creek and raised on stilts. The house can be accessed via a bridge and the large windows and openings offer views through the treetops. The bridge also doubles up as a terrace. The cabin houses a living-dining-kitchen space and a bathroom and functions as a peaceful holiday home or weekend retreat. The wood is treated with Carbonileo, a dark oil that helps to protects the wood. The house adapts to the slope and makes the most of its environment, capturing views of the forest and the sky.

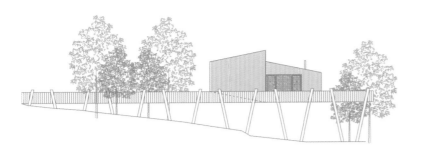

14.5 m² living
9.5 m² sleeping
3.5 m² kitchen
3.5 m² bathrooms
24 m² terrace

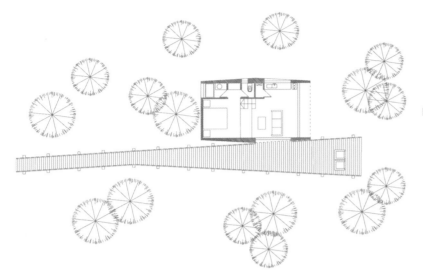

Largely white interiors contrast the surrounding forest scenery.

389

HOUSE NEAR THE HARBOR

Architect | Keggenhoff | Partner
Interior design | Keggenhoff | Partner
Gross floor area | 1,010 m²
Address | Mallorca, Spain
Completion | 2013

The concept behind this design was to develop a 'meeting place' in close proximity to the sea on the south-west side of Mallorca. A refuge was built that would also serve as a meeting place for friends and family. The cubic form of the house contrasts the rough appearance of the nearby coastline. The main focus of the design was the provision of a tranquil place in which to relax. The living area, guest suite, and indoor and outdoor kitchens are all located on the ground floor, while the technical equipment and services are housed in the basement. The private rooms, fitness and wellness areas can be found on the upper floor. Lounges and a large table form an outdoor gathering space.

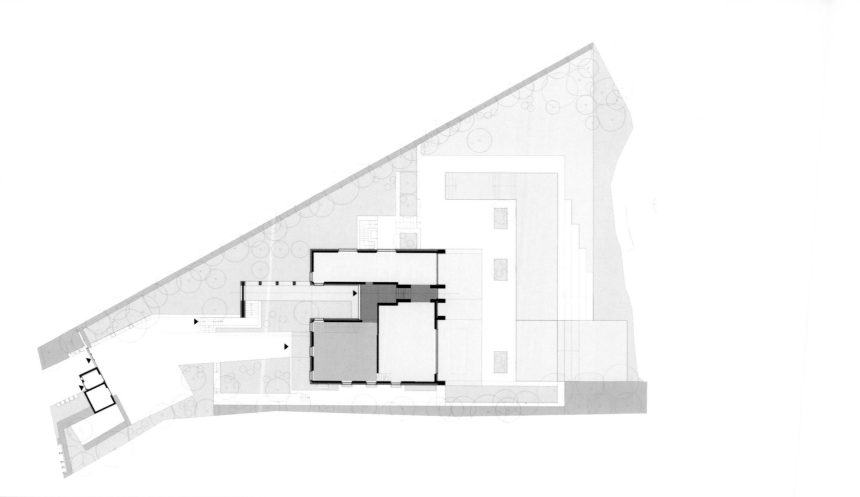

The use of solid natural stone responds to the environment, reflecting the power of the Mediterranean Sea and the solid mass of the cliffs along the coast.

This apartment is organized in two parts, more communal areas for use during the day and private areas housing the bathroom and bedroom. The service spaces are hidden in a cube at the center of the space, which also houses a kitchenette. The kitchenette is divided from the living area by lamella that separate the different functions. Specially designed lighting elements are integrated into the suspended ceiling. The rather clinical atmosphere of straight lines and hard edges is contrasted by the soft curving lines of the furniture.

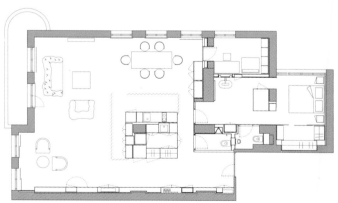

63 m² living
8 m² sleeping
8 m² kitchen
11 m² bathrooms
16 m² entrance
8 m² library

HSV APARTMENT

Is it a clinic? No. Is it a stage set for a new science fiction film? No. Is it an ultra modern apartment in Ljubljana's city center stimulating curiosity? Yes.

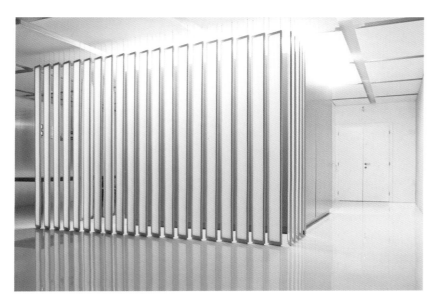

Architect | Sadar+Vuga
Interior design | Sadar+Vuga
Gross floor area | 130 m²
Address | Dukič apartment building, City Center, Ljubljana, Slovenia
Completion | 2012
Number of residents | 1 adult

Different atmospheres are created by lighting. The warm morning atmosphere with sunlit floors becomes mysterious at night when illuminated by the graphic network of ceiling lights.

WALLABY LANE HOUSE

Modern living in the heart of the Australian Bush.

Architect | Robinson Architects
Interior design | Robinson Architects
Gross floor area | 215 m²
Address | Wallaby Lane, Tinbeerwah, Australia
Completion | 2013
Number of residents | 2 adults, 1 child

Wallaby Lane House and Studio are located at Tinbeerwah on the Sunshine Coast. The dwellings were designed by Jolyon Robinson of Robinson Architects for a family relocating from Sydney. The site covers an area of just over 20,000 square meters. Established bush land in the center of the property separates the two buildings. The property is not serviced by town water or sewerage. An onsite wastewater treatment system serves both buildings and harvests rainwater. The house sits high on the site follows the natural contours of the land. Orientated to the north, large eaves and a fly-over roof shade the building. A key focus was placed on cross ventilation, natural daylighting and emphasizing the beautiful views of Cooroy Mountain.

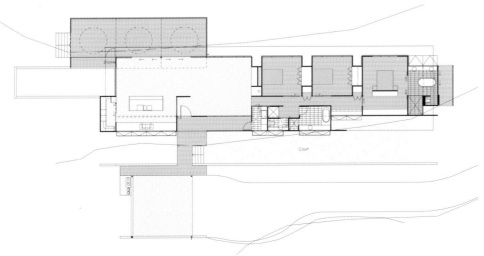

90 m² living and dining
59 m² sleeping
12 m² square

ABOVE THE ROOFS OF FRANKFURT

Maybe not quite a stairway to heaven, but this heavenly stairway is a real focal point of the design.

Interior design | Kern-Design InnenArchitektur
Gross floor area | 340 m²
Address | Schumannstraße 24, 60323 Frankfurt/Main, Germany
Completion | 2011
Number of residents | 2 adults

110 m² living
50 m² sleeping
52 m² kitchen
40 m² bathrooms

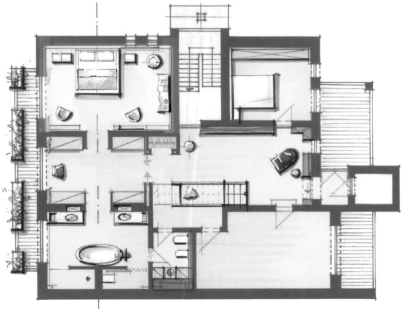

Rising above the roofs of Frankfurt and offering stunning panoramic views of the city skyline, this light-flooded penthouse is perched on the roof of a tall building. Access to the penthouse is provided via an exterior elevator. The client demanded the development of a clear spatial concept that would emphasize both the size of the space and offer a clear division into zones. The staircase forms an important connecting feature on both levels, designed not just as a functional object but also almost as an independent sculpture. The bedrooms, spa bathroom, guest rooms and library are all located on the lower level, while the kitchen, living and dining areas, as well as a cinema can all be found on the upper floor.

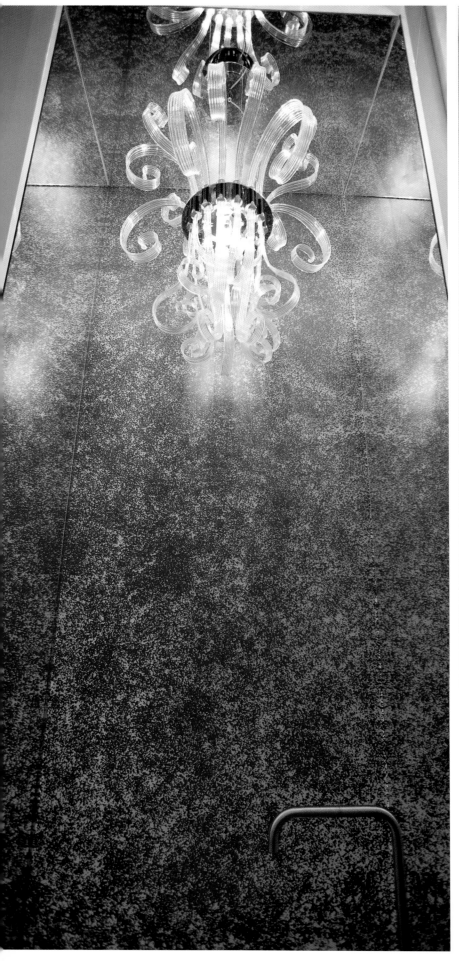

405

The conceptual idea behind this design was the creation of 'spatial flexibility', merged with northern-European style. The client desired a dining area, study and guest room, all integrated into an open-plan space. Thus a space was created that has been segregated to form various functional areas. In accordance with typical northern-European style, most of the main building materials are light in color and include the use of pinewood, Paulownia wood and Pandomo flooring. Decorative elements such as glazed tiles, metallic accessories and colorful fabric give the interior design a playful and colorful accent.

CHEN RESIDENCE

Chilled, bright, light and laid-back – the perfect
example of northern-European flair.

Architect | KC design studio
Interior design | KC design studio
Gross floor area | 69 m²
Address | 12 Shidong Road, Taipei City 111, Taiwan, China
Completion | 2013
Number of residents | 2 adults

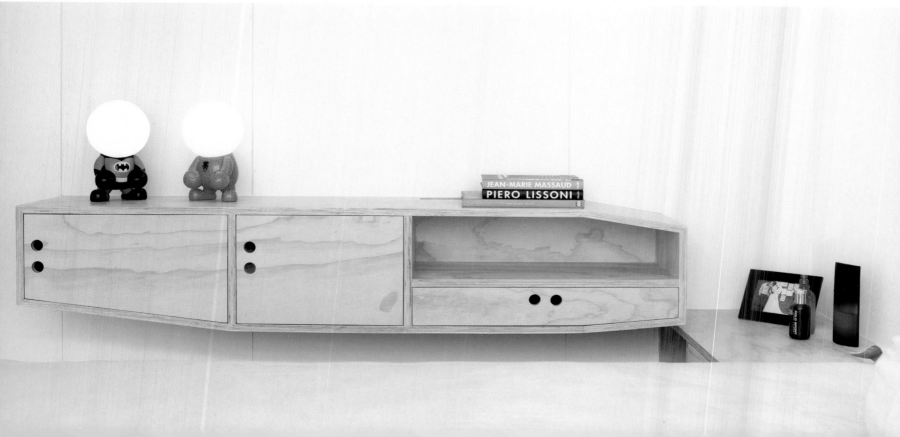

17 m² living
20 m² sleeping
7 m² kitchen
18 m² bathrooms

SCENOGRAPHY

An explosion of light and color, this design is like the Big Bang for housing design.

Architect | aa studio
Interior design | aa studio
Gross floor area | 400 m²
Address | Strada Modrogan 4A, Bucharest, Romania
Completion | 2008
Number of residents | 2 adults

This apartment has an individual character, achieved from and through light. It establishes a strong relationship with the outdoors through a large number of windows. The owner can choose to have these open, flooding the apartment with light, or closed to enjoy the numerous lighting systems. The designers paid special attention to how the lighting transforms and characterizes the space. There are a lot of artificial lighting systems that play with colors, shadows and shades, these work together with the different white surfaces and the curtains that define or close the space.

80 m² living
96 m² sleeping
30 m² kitchen
42.5 m² bathrooms

This 180-square-meter residential house was built in 2004 and renovated and refurnished in 2013. The clients worked closely together with the interior architects in order to ensure that various much-loved pieces were incorporated into the new design. The cupboards built into the sloping ceiling on the upper floor create a wealth of storage space. The selected colors and materials give the space an overall more peaceful and harmonious character. The lighting design also plays an important role in defining the individual areas and developing a variety of atmospheres.

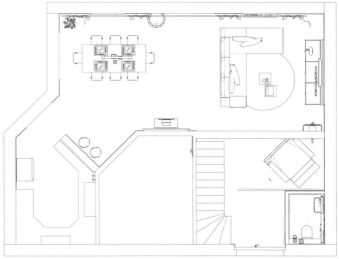

REDESIGN OF APARTMENT IN MÖNCHENGLADBACH

Designed for a real VW Beetle enthusiast.

Architect | raum.atelier
Gross floor area | 600 m²
Address | 41066 Mönchengladbach, Germany
Completion | 2013
Number of residents | 2 adults

The clever storage elements built into this design leave enough leftover space for a car to be integrated into the living room layout.

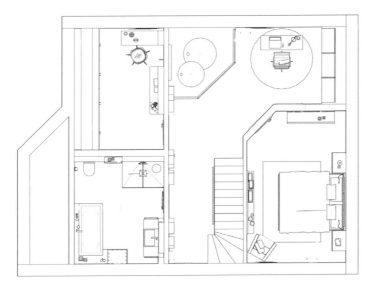

42,20 m² open-plan living
17.40 m² sleeping
14.9 m² kitchen
11.60 m² bathrooms

FAR POND

Wet and wild! This striking design makes the most of views over the wetlands.

Architect | Bates Masi + Architects
Gross floor area | 290 m²
Address | Southampton, NY 11968, USA
Completion | 2012
Number of residents | 1 adult

The waterfront site overlooks layers of wetlands and offers views over the estuary, bay, and the ocean. The existing house was built in the 1970s, and the client expressed a wish to maintain the existing structure while doubling the size of the house with an extension. The existing house clearly expressed the structural system, and it was decided that the extension should also do this. The new system utilizes prefabricated elements that resolve multiple structural and spatial problems. Reducing the use of structural components minimized construction waste.

76 m² living
37 m² sleeping
30 m² kitchen
16 m² bathrooms

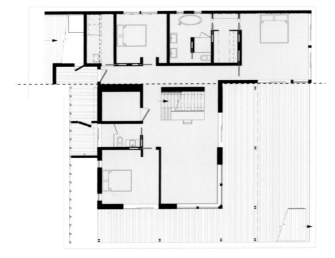

The architects investigated the use of prefabricated shear wall panels, used in light frame construction in areas that are hurricane prone with high force winds. Most are made from a light gauge metal that has been folded to add strength and make it more rigid. A standard light gauge steel sheet has been folded back and forth along the long axis increasing strength and rigidity of the panel. The resulting panel locks into adjacent panels and not only offers structural stability, but also functions as a decorative component.

The building that houses Casa Son Vida is composed of old and new sections. The stunning architecture of the new extension inspired architect Marcel Wanders to complement the building with a highly exclusive, captivating interior, linking old and new. The round and square shapes, soft blobs and new antiques unite the architecture and the interior design. A mixture of traditional and modern references characterizes the villa, from the classic profiled wall lining the curved space to the newly custom-designed cupboards in straight lines. The use contrasting surfaces and the playful interaction between space and dimensions create a unique atmosphere.

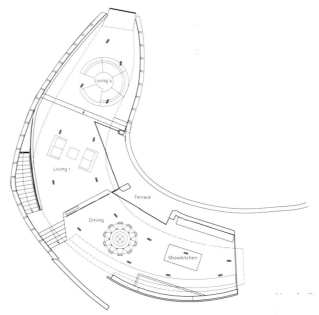

CASA SON VIDA

Catch a glimpse of a futuristic world, where strange organic forms grow down from floating ceilings and where the walls are made of gold.

Architect | TecArchitecture
Interior design | Marcel Wanders
Gross floor area | 800 m²
Address | Palma de Mallorca, Spain
Completion | 2009

TUNQUEN HOUSE

What a panorama! Enjoy an eagle's-eye view of the world below from this lovely getaway.

Architect | Masfernandez Arquitectos
Co-architect | Francisca Ruiz, Rodrigo O'Ryan
Gross floor area | 102 m²
Address | Loteo Punta de Gallo, Parcela 11, Tunquen, Chile
Completion | 2013
Number of residents | 1 adult

The design of this house was controlled by its location, as it was important to protect the building from the wind. Pine wood beams support the structure and almost give the impression that they are embracing the house. A large balcony makes the most of the views of the sea and nearby cliffs. A large window and glass door separate the living area from the balcony, effectively making the exterior space an integral part of the design and extension of the living space. The building's small volume means that it has a minimal impact on the surrounding environment, its gray color shares a dialogue with the nearby cliffs.

20 m² living
54 m² sleeping
18 m² kitchen
10 m² bathrooms
50 m² terrace

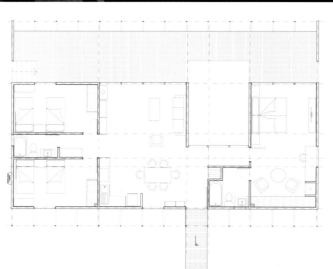

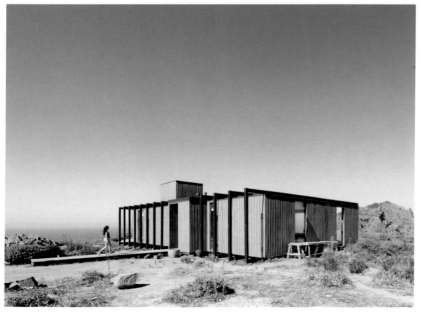

Pine was used not only for the framework (black) and the exterior skin (grey) but also for the interior walls (white).

According to the statistics, the quantity of total housing area in Vietnam has increased tenfold in the last decade. However, many families are still living in very small houses, some of which are less than ten square meters. It is an important issue for Vietnam to provide houses for low-income classes. The aim of this project is to propose a prototype house for low-income families in the Mekong Delta area. Two prototypes were experimentally constructed in Dong Nai province, on the construction site of a kindergarten project designed by Vo Trong Nghia Architects. The first house, with a floor area of 22.5 square meters, was designed as a model home, the second, measuring 18 square meters, was designed as a site office for the kindergarten, showing the flexibility of this prototype.

430

LOW COST HOUSE

Grow your own house. This bamboo house is not
only economical, it's eco-friendly too.

Architect | Vo Trong Nghia Architects
Interior design | Vo Trong Nghia Architects
Gross floor area | 18 m²
Address | Dong Nai province, Vietnam
Completion | 2012
Number of residents | 2 adults, 2 children

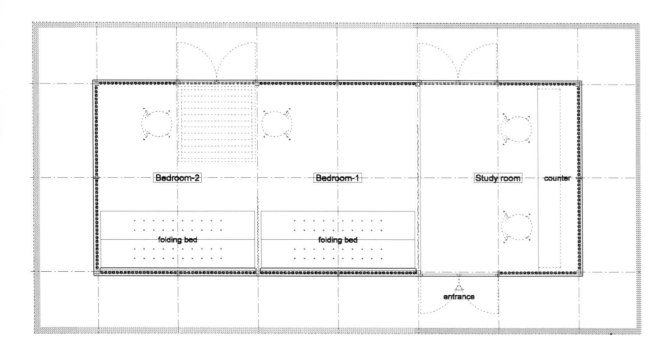

Bedroom-2   Bedroom-1   Study room   counter

folding bed   folding bed

entrance

The envelope of the house is composed of a polycarbonate panel wall and corrugated fiberglass reinforced plastic panel roof, with bamboo louvers set inside. The materials are available everywhere in Vietnam and they are cheap, light and replaceable. Bamboo is a rapid-growing and therefore eco-friendly material.

433

ONE RINCON HILL

This house works like a camera; framing stunning views of the San Francisco cityscape.

Interior design | Mary Ann Gabriele Schicketanz
Gross floor area | 169 m²
Address | San Francisco, CA, USA
Completion | 2009
Number of residents | 2 adults

This high-rise apartment in San Francisco was designed for a retired couple downsizing from a large home. The original three-bedroom, two-bathroom layout had a poor sense of entry, no place to retreat, small bedrooms, and several narrow hallways. The couple's world class photography collection became the source of inspiration for the interior design of their new home. The wall color and fabric palette were chosen to be the perfect backdrop and complement to the art. The new master suite was finished in a more romantic approach with pastel colors and more traditional furnishings. The ceilings were finished in a high gloss to create the illusion of additional height.

38.5 m² living and dining
38.9 m² sleeping
18.5 m² kitchen
25.5 m² bathrooms
20 m² entrance area
27.8 m² master sitting room

435

Silk and wool rugs, rich woods and a large Mica pendant by McEwan Lighting Studio all contribute to the comfort of the client's new home without compromising the modern architecture.

This apartment was built 50 years ago and is located near Paulista Avenue, one of Brazil's more affluent business centers. The original floor plan was modified to better suit the needs of the new user. The apartment has good natural insulation and a lighting system that makes use of fluorescent lamps and directional spots to emphasize different aspects of the design. Brazilian designers, such as Marcus Ferreira, made some of the furniture and textiles used for the old chairs in the dining room were designed by Adriana Barra. The artwork was made by 'Nove' digital organico.

RO APARTMENT

A riot of exploding colors, this house just screams
the spirit of Brazil.

Architect | SuperLimão Studio
Interior design | SuperLimão Studio
Gross floor area | 218.45 m²
Address | Peixoto Gomide 724, São Paulo, Brazil
Completion | 2013
Number of residents | 2 adults

The clients colorful clothes and Brazilian lifestyle inspired the architects to create a colorful and open space. The entire design uses more than 40 colors in total.

88.82 m² living
41.95 m² sleeping
41.94 m² kitchen
25.45 m² bathrooms
20.34 m² corridors

BEGOVAYA

You can look but you can't touch. And please,
please don't scratch anything!

Architect | Geometrix Design
Gross floor area | 93 m²
Address | Moscow, Russia
Completion | 2013

The shiny interior and the stark contrast between black and white certainly give this apartment character. Nothing here has been left to chance. The decorative Neo-Baroque furnishings are complimented by the swirling patterns on the floor, and everything is reflected in the shining surfaces of the cupboards, doors and walls. It is almost like being in a hall of mirrors; with the twirling decorative elements reverberating back at you from the walls, ceilings and floors. The lighting has also been carefully designed to add a new dimension to the white and black furnishings. A large lamp casts a cold blue light over the living room, while other areas are illuminated by varying tones of pink and purple.

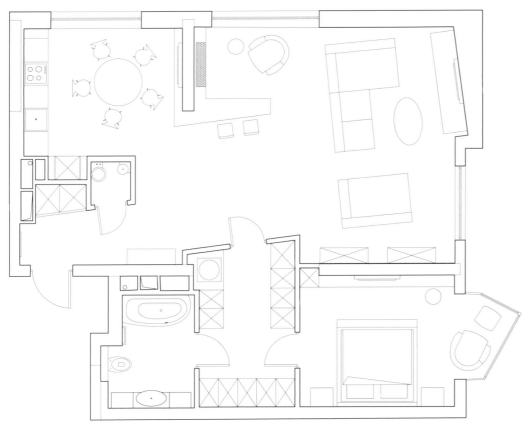

This design brings new life to Neo-Baroque. Symmetrical swirling patterns characterize the design throughout, contrasted here and there by straight-edged suggestions of Art Deco.

This house makes effective use of solid wood panels both inside and outside. The terrace is sheltered from the sun by these planks, which vary in length. Sections of bamboo stems stick out of the plaster, giving the house a somewhat spikey appearance, reminiscent of the small pieces of driftwood and other materials that one finds washed up on a beach. Solid wooden panels are also used inside, which helps to create a dialogue between interior and exterior areas; this is also underlined by large windows and doors that frame views of the ocean and help to draw light inside. Inside, yellow and white walls are combined with colorful artworks, giving the interior a welcoming and friendly appearance.

90 m² living
50 m² sleeping
43 m² kitchen
40 m² bathrooms

RAYBAN HOUSE

Is it a hedgehog? Is it a ruin? No, it's a small house
with a big heart.

Architect | Alejandro D'Acosta Lopez and Claudia Turrent Riquelme
Interior design | Alejandro D'Acosta Lopez and Claudia Turrent Riquelme
Co-architect | Miguel Angel Cuesta Ortega
Gross floor area | 288 m²
Address | Ensenada, Baja California, Mexico
Completion | 2008
Number of residents | 4 adults

INDEX

451

INDEX

IMPRINT

The Deutsche Nationalbibliothek lists this publication in the Deutsche Nationalbiblio-
grafie; detailed bibliographic data are available in the Internet at http://dnb.dnb.de

ISBN 978-3-03768-177-0
© 2015 by Braun Publishing AG
www.braun-publishing.ch

1st edition 2015

Editor: Editorial Office van Uffelen
Editorial staff and layout: Christina Mihajlovski, Lisa Rogers, Johanna Schröder
Graphic concept: Michaela Prinz, Berlin
Reproduction: Bild1Druck GmbH, Berlin